good deed rain

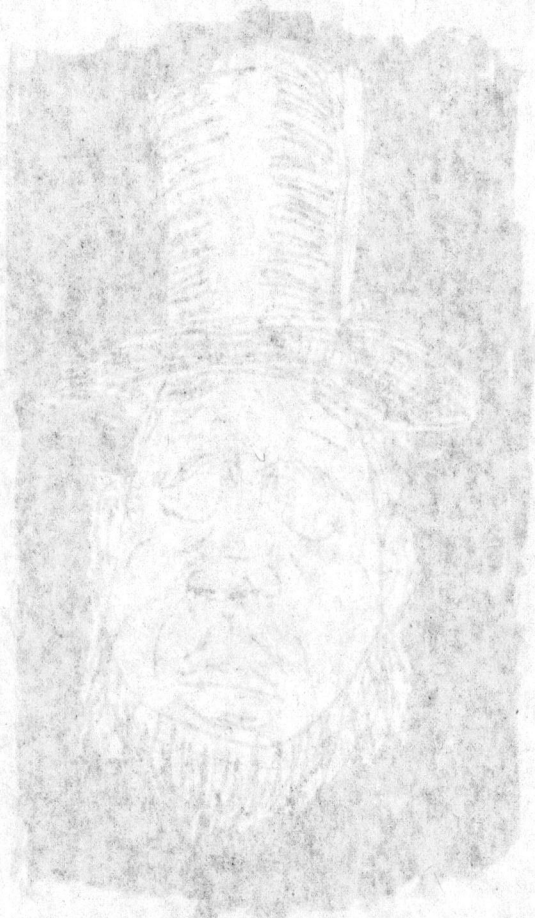

one

drop

in

the

milky way

One Drop in the Milky Way © 2023
Allen Frost, Good Deed Rain
Bellingham, Washington
ISBN: 978-1-0882-5618-3

Writing: Allen Frost
Cover Illustration: Aaron Gunderson
Cover Production: Priya Shalauta
Quotes:
Return from Witch Mountain, Alexander Key, Pocket
Books, NY, 1978.
Your Next Ten Years: Criswell Predicts, Droke House
Publishers, 1969.
White Noise, Don DeLillo, Viking Press, NY, 1985.
Apple: TFK!

"I'm from another world where people would never
dream of treating each other the way they do here."
        —*Return from Witch Mountain*

"This world and every item in it is duplicated a trillion
times over in the vast universe of nearby space!
Why should you feel lonely when you have a trillion
counterparts?"
        —Criswell

ONE DROP
in the
MILKY WAY

by Allen Frost

Good Deed Rain ◊ Bellingham, Washington ◊ 2023

I am the false character that follows the name around.

—*White Noise*

INTRODUCTION

Would you be surprised to see a skeleton walking along the sidewalk? I wonder if anyone would—in this time it doesn't seem such a shock. What would catch the attention of this modern audience of ours? What if Abraham Lincoln was added next to him? When the two of them walk the city streets they fit right in with America, treated to haunted flapjacks and free coffee, ready to face the day, and if there's a way to repair the damage that's been done, they will find it.

A.F, August 2023

The CHAPTERS

Infinite Wisdom

Nothing

Dream Animals

Burnt Coffee

Catching Sunlight

Chandu the Magician

The Grand Scheme of Things

The Set to Pop Parking Lot

Forgiven

The Movie with Fay Wray

Other Planes of Existence

World Without End

CHAPTER 1

The TOWN HEEL

When I was ten, I didn't worry about who I would be, who I would become in the 21st Century was an unquestioned mystery. If I have turned out in ways I couldn't imagine, sorry kid, you had no idea what lay before you. And neither did this older me. I made a mistake. I sure didn't expect to be in this situation. There are struggles and pitfalls and pressures the puppets and songs on the *June on the Moon* TV show don't prepare you for. But I didn't know that when I was ten.

I tried to play it safe. The only other time I had trouble with the law, I was still in grade school—I was late for my job and I ran across the Ave. A cop was waiting for me on the curb. He gave me a ticket for jaywalking. I got a court date and a counselor to talk to. I went to the police department to plead my case. A man waited for me in an office. He was surrounded by paper stacks and file folders. A cigarette in an overcrowded ashtray. He took one look at me and said, "Consider yourself counseled and released." I was lucky, I got off easy. That should have been a lesson.

Now I'm a fugitive. It would be simple to join the crowds of homeless on the street. People hurry around them every day. I could sit with my back to a wall and go not-so-slowly crazy. I didn't want to end up living by the creek in a culvert with the skunk cabbages. Instead, I live on campus in the walls of Old Main. Well, not quite—I followed the crawlspace up to the attic—that's where I sleep at night. I have a candle, a book, and a polar bear skin on a pallet. Nice as it is, I promise I'll find a better place. I can't stay here forever. I don't want to become the Phantom of the Opera.

On the 1st floor of Old Main, on the west side, if you walk to the middle of the hall, you'll find what looks like the hatch of a laundry chute. Don't ask me how I got the key to the lock. Alright, I bribed a janitor. Add it to my rap sheet. Anyway, I'm sure it hasn't been opened by anyone else since the early seventies. I don't enter the building until long after nightfall. Another key, another bribe. I'll admit it, I'm the town heel. But does that mean I deserve all this grief?

What do I need to do? There must be someone who could show me the way. I know an English teacher who wanted to be a detective. She was taking night classes after work. For some reason, along the way she gave up on her dream. Something about it wasn't right, but quitting left her with regret. Mornings I would see her carrying essays to the Humanities building and she would sigh, "I should have stayed with it. They had us examine actual crime scenes. I was good at it." That's what detectives do—go through clues and find justice. I could ask her advice. If it was easy as apologizing, I would do that. Put me in front of everyone at a big assembly in the gym. I could handle the booing. I would put my heart into my speech. I would lean close to the microphone, "Webster's Dictionary defines *Sorry* as—" More jeering and buried in the crowd, a clap as the English teacher slaps her forehead.

Old Main is like a tomb at night. The lights are off. I rely on the moonlight in the windows. When I get to the hatch, I start my climb between the walls, up a hundred feet to the rafters. It sounds like it couldn't get much worse for me, but you wouldn't believe what I've gone through already. It's a miracle I'm surviving day to day. If you're interested in the story, I guess this is a good time to start…at the beginning…

CHAPTER 2

LAST RESORT

...when I realized I was getting close to retirement. It creeps up on you. It seems true I've been part of the same universal cycle at this school up here on the hill—like me, the students put in their years, stamped in the sight of this place, then suddenly they're shipped out. I've seen it happen again and again. They're happy enough hopefully and then they're gone. There's not much difference between us and the salmon coming and going in Pardon Creek. Have I been at it this long? Apparently. So while I'm excited about the next step, I need to find out how I'll make ends meet. It needed percolating. I had to sleep on it.

Then, suddenly, I had the idea! I'm surprised nobody else thought of it. I can't be the only one with such a devious mind. I thought of a good way to make some money, maybe a lot of it, and like most plans of that nature, it was nefarious. It was a risk I was willing to take.

How does it feel to be the greatest traitor this school has ever known? First of all, is that strictly true? Surely there must be someone worse than me. I mean, all I did was ruin the chances of a sports team. Is that so bad? All I had was a good idea that verged on the criminal, that proved to be the wrong thing to do.

Am I trying to sound like a decent person? I hope so. All I've done is what anyone would do— sorry...not *anyone*—our founding father George Washington would never stoop to my level. He would have tossed me right out of his picturesque boat. I would have blubbered and begged for rescue as I sank in the Potomac waves.

The next morning after my visionary dream, I went to Radio Shack and bought their smallest film camera. I hope you readers are prepared for the horrible thing I did. Seems like a lot of buildup. I hid a Secret Spy camera high on the wall of Carver

Gym by one of the beams. Only a seven-year-old would take the time to look for it.

I filmed the basketball team practicing. My film showed all their plays and shouted codes. I knew it would be gold to their opponents. I sent copies to Cal State, Western Oregon, Barry University, East Bay Baptist, the Academy of Art, Central Washington, and Armstrong State University. It turned out it wasn't gold. They all told me the same thing in so many words, "We can't take this, it's criminal." The videos came back to me, but that doesn't mean they didn't watch them. I'm not accusing them of doing that, it's just curious that we went on to have our worst season ever.

Those other schools got their cake and ate it too.

I'm not that lucky. I got stuck with the rap. And I didn't make a penny.

I'm aware of the newspapers. *The Bugle* and *The Shopper's Gazette*. I find *The Herald* in the bin every night and read it. I can tell what I'm thought of. They're unforgiving. When the story broke—how I sold out our team—it was bad. What could I do, how could I explain? I'm not exactly innocent, that half of the story is true. If only I could out-survive *The Herald*'s coverage, I had to hope for a disaster that would eclipse me.

The school newspaper was especially cruel. They pilloried me on the front-page. I was despicable, I was the sort of villain you read about in the pulps. I ruined the chances for the basketball team. They lost game after game, once the pride of the school, once champions of the NCAA league. Worst of all, the school fired our beloved Coach Wooden because of my interfering. Sure, he was reinstated when my treason was discovered, but I was the cause of their humiliating season and he had it in for me. And believe me, if you've seen him in action, pacing the court, screaming at the ref, raving like a maniac, you don't want him targeting you.

The university fired me. Retired me early is how I prefer to think of it, without pay.

That same day, my landlord evicted me. The news traveled fast.

Where could I turn?

Everything from my apartment was piled on the lawn.

I was terrified.

I didn't know where to go…The Aloha Motel?

That's a last resort…I live in a small world, the only other place I could think of going was work. Sad, I know. Sorry if my mind is spinning round and round, that's the way it works now. Up the hill to Old Main and in.

I had a last resort. I live in a small world, the
only other place I could think of going is work.
Sad, I know. Sorry if my mind is spinning round
and around, that's the way it works now. Up the hill
to Old what's-it by...

CHAPTER 3

PURGATORY

I'm surrounded by stacks of boxes and steamer trunks, furniture and picture frames, everything you would expect to be stored in a hundred-year-old attic. There are forgotten things around here everywhere. My pillow is a zippered bag holding an old raccoon coat that would suit Rudy Vallee. But not me. I've looked in some of the boxes, I've got plenty of time up here to do that. I found a box full of old games. There's a French one called Mille Bornes. I'm still reading up on the rules. Something about automobiles. Then it came to me—another one of my great ideas arrived in the next trunk I looked in.

The steamer was labeled DRAMA DEPT. And the contents were something else. I discovered exactly what I needed for the new me. Not at first though. A straw boater hat, a pinstripe suit, two-tone leather shoes, a yellow wig and moustache. Nobody would suspect it was me, but I would look like a P.G. Wodehouse fool.

I wasn't ready for that challenge.

I pushed it aside and dug further and then there it was—I found my perfect disguise.

In the morning I would reveal myself to the world. There was no immediate rush. If I could sleep through the first winter night, I would be thankful. It's cold up here, even wrapped in a polar bear skin. I'm willing to believe an igloo would be warmer. An igloo built of fitted blocks no wind could whistle through, with a seal oil lamp making golden light on the curved walls. A husky dog on my feet, a warm partner beside me under blankets made of fur, the aurora borealis whirling colors overhead, all the luxuries of a world less inhospitable.

That's how it is in the attic of Old Main. I got used to it.

Well, I'm not alone anyway. I just heard a rat.

Let's hope that's all it was. I know there's supposed to be a ghost in Old Main. Who was it again? A secretary on a spirit typewriter, or a teacher grading endless tests? There was an article in the *The Bugle*, I can't remember the details. I suppose if I meet the ghost, I'll know more. Until then, I have to content myself with the rats.

It does occur to me, I'm in prime position to become the next ghost here. If anything goes wrong one of these nights, a very real possibility, I'll be doomed to these rafters until my purgatory service is through. Until I've earned it, I guess. And if I don't make it and I'm stuck here, I can lend a ghostly hand filing reports from 1957, important documents that still exist in another dimension, or I can help proofread essays written on an endless Mobius strip.

Yes, that's a rat alright. It's chewing on something over there. A rolled-up map maybe. I reached for anything I could throw at it. They do this all night, running back and forth on the crossbeams just out of reach, gnawing on an infinite supply of university history.

I yelled and threw my shoe at the darkness.

After the crash, it was suddenly quiet.

I wish I picked a better artifact to throw. I would need my shoe...Hadn't I lost enough? Then I thought of the rat crawling out of its hiding place. Pretty soon I'd hear it chewing my shoe. By morning there'd be nothing left but eyelets. I didn't want to, but I knew I had to look for the shoe. I patted my hand around the candle next to my pallet until I found the matches.

With a snap, I touched the match to the wick and I held a little lighthouse.

When I moved into Old Main's attic, the first thing I did was cover the windows at each end. A candle would make an eerie faint glow if anyone happened to look up. That's how ghost rumors get started.

I moved slowly and carefully along the beam. I can't avoid creaking those old timbers, but I try my best to be quiet. Below me are offices. The custodians won't be in the building until 3 AM but you never know. Did I say I try my best to be quiet? Yeah...when I'm not throwing my shoe. That was a mistake. I had to learn the hard way not to make them. That's putting it lightly.

My knees aren't made for this anymore. Were they ever? Sure, when I was ten and climbing branches and making treehouses out of slats of scrapwood. I could do just about anything then, practically fly along the sidewalks fearlessly.

The candle made shadows of the trunks ahead of me. Boxes full of paper rolls sticking in the air like flower stems. Fortunately I wouldn't be gardening all night—my shoe rested against a cardboard dent. I was lucky I wouldn't spend the rest of midnight looking for it.

Not to brag, but my aim had been good. Coach Wooden would have thought so too. Right next to my shoe was the rat's gnawed scroll. It had bent down free of the box. As I neared and the candlelight revealed more from the murk, I realized what I had found.

I was looking for a way out of my predicament, but I never expected a rat to show me the way.

CHAPTER 4

A
NEW
AQUAINTANCE

Setting the candle down on the edge of a dusty trunk, I unrolled the paper tube. I wanted to believe it would be a treasure map. After all I've been through, a reward would be nice. The parchment was old enough to be something a pirate would leave behind, but I didn't see any shoals or a shore with a dotted line leading into the woods where a red X was planted. In fact, the paper was blank until I reached the middle. Spelled in faded ink were the words: *Lucky Skeleton*. An arrow pointed to the right and two more words followed: *in casket*.

The candle flickered. We both held our breath for a moment. Can a candle hold its breath? This one did. With its flame calmed, I took a step and moved the light in the direction of the arrow. Although I've taken up residence in the attic, there are great regions I haven't explored. I haven't been to Pittsburgh either.

I don't know if the darkness I was approaching could compare with the City of Bridges and its famous botanical gardens, by candlelight it was hard to tell. Fortunately, the inhabitants of this strange land had laid down sheets of plywood over the rafters so it wasn't as dangerous to traverse. I found myself in a narrow canyon of stacked boxes and ventured on. No sign of a casket yet. Was I being courageous or foolhardy, I don't know. But at this point in my life I could use a little luck, even if it was a skeleton.

The crooked path led me on further between the tall cardboard walls. Hopefully the way hadn't been carved through by a minotaur. I brushed another spiderweb aside. If this was a fairytale, I should've been laying down a trail of crumbs behind me. Of course, the rats would approve of that plan. Once upon a time in the Black Forest, these same shadows walked, with witches and wolves, while the hungry birds made sure Hansel and Gretel were truly lost.

I'm not in quite the same danger I don't think. Or if I am, I haven't yet reached the candy cottage or the ominous grandmother with very sharp teeth. I don't scare easily, but now, edging my way through this tomb looking for a skeleton's coffin gave me reason to be. Another spiderweb singed my cheek.

Can Old Main go much further? Was the wooden floor extending out beyond the treetops, were there clouds under me taking me across the sea to Japan? I was afraid if I looked overhead, I would see haunted stars. Just as I was thinking that, the path ended, stoppered by a casket pushed against the eaves.

It looked perfect in the candlelight. If Bela Lugosi was waiting for his cue, this was it.

Okay.

What did I have to lose?

I set the candle on the floor and opened the lid.

For a brief moment it seemed filled with black water. Wait—what was in it? A dolphin? There was something in that ink. I bent to retrieve the candle and when I returned with that meager light, a skeleton was sitting up in the cetaceous casket. It lifted a bony arm and said, "Hiya sport."

That would be a good place to end this chapter, with me dropping the candle and everything going pitch black, but he wasn't done talking. I would find that mandible rarely ever tired. It opened and his voice clacked out, "What took you so long?"

Was I surprised? In my dire life of late, I've become used to many things I've been forced to endure. A talking skeleton was actually acceptable to me. "I'm guessing you're the lucky skeleton?" I asked.

"Lucky's my name," he replied. "A skeleton is what I am."

"I see that."

"What about you?" he asked, "You got a name?"

"Howard Harvard."

"Nice to meet you, How." He stuck out a spidery grasp of metacarpals and phalanges and we shook hands.

It was a little strange, not what you'd expect from a living thing. I could see right through him.

Lucky grinned, or maybe he always did, "So what happened anyway? What brings you to this real estate?"

"Well…" I took a deep breath and told Lucky Skeleton my story.

CHAPTER 5

A FIBONACCI SPIRAL

I've worked at the university for going on twenty-five years. What do I do for a job? What a lot of Americans do, I suppose. I stare at a computer and enter letters and numbers. How's that sound? Funny thing is, each letter or number affects someone, some student or someone somewhere at this school and beyond. Monday through Friday, each week fills a calendar that falls to the side as I slide on by. It felt like there was no end, day after day, building forever in a Fibonacci spiral. Hard to believe. And now I'm tired. I was ready to be retired. But I guess I blew that.

When you start planning for retirement, the first thing you do is look at numbers. How much is your current salary and earnings, what are your benefits and deductions, how about health insurance?—it might be the last time you have to do such strenuous thinking. And they know it, they've got you on the ropes. At least that's how it felt. And all that stress of imaginary tornado flattened me and left me with the realization that I didn't have a fortune to get by on. Think of something to supplement your income, they told me. I know someone from work who has an oil derrick in his backyard. It hasn't found oil yet, but it continues to dip at the ground. Stay active, try volunteering, there are lots of charities in town. Those connections can lead to something else. The city is always looking for part-time workers to count cars or tag pigeons or get signatures. Some of those jobs pay well. Sure they do. The casinos are hiring too, I could empty ashtrays.

When I left Human Resources after that exhausting meeting, I realized I had to come up with something else. Something that would actually fill a bucket for a rainy day. I didn't know what that would be until I stopped at the gymnasium on the way back to my office.

Just inside the doors of Carver Gym, on the other wall before you turn in to the basketball court, there's a water fountain with the best water in the city. I call it Wooden Water in honor of Coach Wooden. I pretend he's got a natural spring hooked up to that fountain, chock full of vitamins and suffused with magnetic ions. The Coach has got me over a barrel, I'm pretty much addicted to the stuff. I cross the bricks from my office seven or eight times a day going for water, wet bricks, misty rain, green firs and cedars, gray sky, sound of seagulls.

As I say, that's where I was, filling my bottle with Wooden Water to boil for tea, when my brilliant, devious get-rich scheme became clear.

It's all about survival, right? I mean other things are attached to that, sympathy and empathy, love and caring for the planet, the list goes on, but survival is life. Anyway, that's how I can justify what I did.

I heard sneakers cheeping on the court, the heartbeat thud of a ball. I turned to look at the waxy yellow floor. I saw the team through the doorway, going through drills. Coach Wooden whistled and shouted from the sideline. He held his arms out and motioned like someone in the signal corp. I didn't know what he was doing, guiding the team the way a puppeteer will pull strings, but I guessed if someone from another team was watching, they could decipher our team's code, and learn all our plays. Then I thought of hiding a camera somewhere on the balcony. A few cameras would be good. Then—I'm sorry in hindsight for the fault of my thoughts—I figured I could sell the film to the opposition. For instance, when the Bulldogs arrived here from Ferris State, they could predict our side's every move. All I asked for in return was a little money from each team. If I could get myself a nest egg, I'd be happy. That's all I wanted. Just enough to know I was taken care of in my old age.

After work that day, I took the bus to Radio Shack. I walked past the calculators, doorbells and telephones and every kind of radio. I stopped to look at a car radar detector. How are those legal? It struck me strange that a gadget like that is legitimate. I should have turned around, but I carried on past a row filled with wires and outlets and roller-skates for robots until I reached the camera counter. The big glass case was stocked full.

"Welcome to Radio Shack, can I help you?"

"Hi—" I read the nametag, "...DeRayle. I'm looking for the smallest film camera you have."

"A spy camera?" The kid grinned at me.

"Well, no...but yes."

CHAPTER 6

LOW
TIDE

Lucky Skeleton laughed.

"I know," I said. Let that be a lesson to anyone listening. "I'm detestable."

"No," he shook a bony finger, "I've known a lot of charlatans. At worst, you're just a common variety opportunist."

"Well, thanks, but that's not what the school and everyone in town thinks of me."

He grinned. I guess he was always grinning. "So what happened?"

"I got caught."

He laughed again.

"I made the tapes. That was easy. I had three

cameras hidden in the gym, I even got closeup footage of the playbook. I looked at the season schedule and I mailed letters to each team's coaching staff…Barry University, Florida State, Azusa Pacific, Dowling College, Washburn, Utah Tech. They all took the bait. It almost could have gone my way. The team had its worst losing streak ever. They fired Coach Wooden. I didn't feel good about that. Then someone turned me in." I'm still not sure who discovered my plot, but I was in real trouble…until I got a letter from The Academy of Art…But that comes later on.

"What'd they do?" Lucky leaned his elbows on the edge of the casket. He was intrigued.

"They reported me to the dean."

"Ooooooohh," Lucky's bony hands covered where his eyes would have been.

They sent a black and white cruiser from the school's security force. I was washing the supper dishes. I was listening to a record. It might have been Zoot Sims. I was thinking about watching a movie that night. There was a double feature at the Avalon. That's as far as I got, thinking about it.

There was a knock at the door.

Part of me was waiting for this moment. Part

of me knew that karma would catch up with me. I saw the police car parked by the curb. I backed from the window as the knock continued to pepper the door. If I opened it, they'd take me away. "That's when I became a fugitive."

Lucky asked me, "How long have you lived up here?"

"Gosh, I don't know. A month or two?"

"Sheesh," he said, looking around at the shadows and dark. At least he couldn't smell the surroundings. "Why here?"

"It wasn't my first choice," I told him. There are so many places to hide but here I was. I could keep it going for years if I had to. I hope I don't. I don't want to be the shadow you think you just saw out the corner of your eye. When they came for me that night, I snuck out onto the fire escape and made my way down the iron rungs. They didn't bother stationing an officer in the alley. I guess that didn't make me as wanted as Dillinger. Where could I go at half past six on a winter night? I was halfway down the block when I realized I left the water running in the sink. Even with my mind in such a frantic state of escape, I pictured the police breaking the lock on the door and swinging it open to a flood of soapy waves. Everything in my apartment would wash out in those waves. There would be nothing left in there but low tide. For some reason that was comforting. Low tide…It would follow me for months.

I followed the sidewalk. I stayed close to the shadows dropped by the trees. The hill went up, houses on either side, then down towards town. Over a rooftop, shimmering past the chimney and TV aerial, I could see the neon green and pink glow of the Aloha Motel. Let's just say it has a reputation for the lawless, the derelicts, the homeless, the tempest-tossed, the wretched, the down and out and desperate, in other words, my crowd.

Compared to where I am now, The Aloha could be a 5-star hotel, but it was quite a bit more appalling than my apartment. I won't go into the details, Tolstoy already has, but to its credit for two nights, as long as my money lasted, I was able to hide out there and watch as my world fell apart. My room had a TV and I was the top story. I guess nothing else was happening on planet Earth. I saw my apartment, taped off in yellow tape, a police sketch-artist had drawn a ferocious picture of me.

The camera showed the campus and the office where I worked, my desk torn open where they looked for clues. People were interviewed who knew me and everyone said the same thing. How could I do it? They thought they knew me. Who *was* I?

But terrible as that was, the worst was yet to come. The TV report closed on the basketball court. "This is where it began," the newscaster solemnly announced, staring into the camera at me, "and wherever he might be hiding, Coach Wooden has a special message for Howard Harvard..." Oh, the look on Coach Wooden's face! I don't ever want to see that in three dimensions. He was furious. Even though he had been vindicated, rehired and lauded like Caesar's ghost, he held a grudge. His team bounced around him as he turned from the reporter, held up his fists and snarled into the screen, "When I get my hands on Harvard, I'll tear him apart!"

CHAPTER
7

The
TRAIN
to
TRANSYLVANIA

"I had six dollars left in my pocket when I left the Aloha. I was officially an outlaw." My bank account at the credit union was blocked. I was fired, disgraced, and on the run. I looked at the birds enviously. They perch on fences and branches and the world offers them everything they need: food, shelter, songs to sing. "I followed a blue jay up Rome Hill, away from the neighborhood, into the woods." I wished I could plant my feet in the ground and become a tree. There's a job I could do: creak with the wind. "I followed a steep dirt path. Twice I had to step off it into the cover of ferns and leaves and wait for people walking the other way." It was early morning but there's always someone going to work. Funny, work is where I was going for all these years too, and now I am done. Not exactly the retirement I planned on. "Force of habit was leading me back to where I sunk twenty-five years."

If I could catch all those clouds from the steamplant smokestack and pile them around me, what an arch-criminal that would make me: The Cloud. I'd have my picture on the Post Office wall: WANTED, with some astronomical reward for my capture. It might be worth it to turn myself in and collect that...Careful, I told myself, don't drift too far, I needed my wits.

Through the firs and cedars, I could see the sturdy brick outlines of a building I knew inside and out. The birds could have the rooftop, I just wanted the attic.

It was good that I kept the janitor's key. Originally, I planned on hiding my retirement movie money in the wall of Old Main. Now I'd hide myself in there. I was worse off than The Cloud, I was trapped in a Gothic horror ghosting the walls and halls.

"That's about it," I said. Here I was, holding a

candle, talking to a skeleton seated in a coffin—it was like the train to Transylvania. "That's my story. That's where I stand...I don't know...Maybe I ought to call it quits. It doesn't look like it gets any better." How's it feel to be a spy and a schemer? At the moment, not so good.

"That's where you're wrong, How! I'm your lucky charm, everything's about to change!"

"Really?"

"Sure!" he beamed.

I looked at my hand. The candle holder had the barest bit of light left.

"First of all, you need a different reputation. How about underground hero? Remember Robin Hood? What if it turns out you did it to save a bankrupt orphanage? Something like that."

"Sure..." I yawned. I was getting sleepy. I was hungry too. If I get hungry enough in the middle of the night, there's a vending machine on the second floor. In a nook under the stairwell, it glows blue and white. *Sir Vend* is written in cursive light with a cartoon knight holding a paper cup. I'm partial to the instant Matzo Ball Soup, only 75¢. Not tonight though, I just wanted to get back to my pallet.

Lucky said, "Let's see what I can do. I'm already getting an idea," he spun his bony hands, "Let me tumble it around."

The candle flickered and died. "There goes my light." I stood in pitch black. "How am I supposed to find my way back?"

"That's a cinch," Lucky said. He snapped his fingers and suddenly he was shimmering a pale ghostly green. Like one of those Five and Dime toys, he was glowing in the dark. "Help me out of this crate and I'll guide you."

There's a skeleton in the storage room where I work—where I used to work—and on occasion I had to move it to classrooms. It was anchored by a pole to a wheeled platform. Anyone I passed in the hall would have something to say, some joke to make light of me walking Death.

"That's better," said Lucky as his feet touched the floor. "I've been cooped up far too long, it's nice to get a little fresh air."

"Fresh air?" I never heard such praise for a hundred-year-old attic.

"You ought to spend a little time in a coffin. Believe me, you'll appreciate the finer things in life."

I did. I do. And I never thought I'd appreciate the glow of a skeleton chaperon either. He actually threw more light than the candle. Following him was easy in the vast gloom.

"Oh look," he said as we turned an abrupt cardboard corner. "There's Seymour."

I don't know if it was the same rat I threw my shoe at, but Seymour took one look at me holding that same shoe again and scampered. "Great," I said. "He's got a name…"

"Certainly. And over there on that beam, that's Richard the fly. We talk all the time. Betty the bat will be around here somewhere too."

"Does everyone have a name?"

"Sure. We're all in this together."

Lucky was right. This big wooden hull wrapped around like Noah's ark is our shelter and transport to the next day's morning light. No one knows what a day may bring. I made my own bed and now I sleep in it.

CHAPTER
8

A
UNIVERSAL
LANGUAGE

I'm reminded I was hired here because of an animal lie. On my application, under the Skills section, I confessed that I could speak to birds. Everyone knows you have to bend the truth a little on these forms. I was lucky there wasn't an ornithologist on the committee. Nobody questioned my outrageous lie at the time, but it's a talent that sure would come in useful in Old Main's attic.

A couple days ago a bird got inside. It must have found a loose slat in a shutter. It was sputtering back and forth frantically. I asked Lucky if he talked to birds too. If I knew a few words, I could have calmed it and shown it the way out. Lucky said anyone could learn.

He called Seymour. The rat scurried onto a box and stared at me.

Lucky asked me, "How...Is there something you want to tell Seymour?"

The rat glared at me.

I took a deep breath and hissed, "Sorry. Sorry I threw that shoe at you."

Turns out I didn't need to say it aloud, it was understood.

The rat stared into my eyes. It knew all about me, it saw everything like a movie, my not-so slow descent into the nocturnal eaves it called home. The rat accepted my apology.

Words didn't reach me in response, words weren't needed for this conversation. I could picture our communication in my mind. Lucky said that's the universal language, once I understood it and practiced it, it works for anyone. You can even talk to a dandelion this way. I haven't tried that yet. Once things settle down maybe I can lie down on a lawn next to one. Not sure what I'll say, but I'll think of something then.

Seymour returned to the darkness. I felt better

about going to sleep, knowing our trouble was sorted. Next time I go to the automat I'll get a bit of cheese for that rat. I should have transmitted that. Oh well, it will be a nice surprise.

"That was a good start," Lucky said. "Your first lesson."

What was I thinking about on the pallet before I fell asleep? Other ways to communicate. Can we send dreams to each other too? Sometimes dreams feel like they're coming off a typewriter or from some film projector I have nothing to do with. I'll be in a place I've never seen, people I don't know, on some mysterious errand. I think I've even been a rat before.

I'd like to blame my dreams for this screwball basketball caper.

The idea really started with a dream. Usually when I wake up from a dream I don't know where I've been, but not this time. It came to me like a postcard. In my dream I had a secret I had to deliver to another school's mascot. I met a tiger in the shadows of a big gymnasium. Like a spy, I handed over the microfilm. A foghorn needed to be blowing. I was about to go when the mascot removed its animal head and revealed the private investigator hired to tail me. He was proud of himself, "Nobody thought I could do it. I had to put in a bid. Admittedly, I'm not the best, just the cheapest. Buy hey, I got you!" I didn't want to hear the life-story of a dream detective. It didn't take much to get away. I hopped a school bus decorated with streamers and painted banners and I got behind the wheel. Anyone who's done this in a dream knows what that can be like—the road was a rollercoaster and the brakes didn't work and I drove right into the sea. The bus became a submarine and a marching band was trapped in the bus with me playing while we flowed in and out of fish and the windows shined underwater. By the time we found land again we were home, the mill towers, smokestacks, the surf, the shore, all the washed-up sand dollars spinning like records. The music had turned into the most beautiful sound I ever heard. I knew what I had to do when I woke up.

CHAPTER 9

TALKING
to a
DOG

My neck is always sore in the morning. In fact, my entire body is suffering from the Old Main amenities. It could be said my mind is going too. One look at my familiar disguise should be proof of that. But how else could I go about in daylight without being mobbed and hauled to the nearest dungeon?

It was raining. I could hear the rain ping in the drainpipe, tapping on the rooftiles like a thousand Fred Astaires up there. The old grandfather clock leaning at a Pisa angle read 6:46. Its gears clicked like the rain. I wasn't keen on leaving my polar bear blanket, the thought of facing another day wasn't that appealing. Still, that's what I do.

By the time Lucky clickety-clacked around the corner of boxes, I was dressed in my disguise and ready for the world.

The skeleton laughed. He has a lot of nerve finding me funny. I don't know when he last checked a mirror. Lucky bowed, one arm tucked below his ribcage, "Mr. Lincoln…"

That's right. I have become Abraham Lincoln.

Old Honest Abe.

The guy on the penny.

You'd be surprised how instantly I'm forgiven when people think I'm him. Suddenly I'm a hero. People give me free coffee, sandwiches at cafés, and even jobs that pay. Just yesterday I was on Iowa Street when a man ran across the car lot to catch me. He begged me to do a spot for his commercial, selling a Chevrolet. He showed me a hundred-dollar bill and I said sure. Dogs run up to fences when they see me, whimpering, wagging their tails. Mothers with babies want my blessing. Bus drivers waive their fares. It's hard to believe this same character lives in hiding when so many people need him around.

Anyway, Lucky said my days as Lincoln were

numbered—he was working on an idea, one he'd been tumbling in his hollow head all dawn. I was ready for a new idea—I had gone as far as I could with mine.

First of all, Lucky and I needed to get out of the building before the office crowd arrived. By now the custodians would have been and gone. We would be the first ones on the buffered floors. A gray blue light ran in the hall, dimmed by all the firs and cedars on Rome Hill. Of course I couldn't turn the lights on, but it was getting easier to see in the morning. Another spring was arriving. I saw our reflection in the windows as we passed the forest. What a strange sight we were. A skeleton and me. Maybe it's the stovepipe hat—it makes me look steam-powered, like a train with a smokestack, at any moment I could be billowing coal.

There's a backdoor at the end of the Old Main basement that opens into a concrete trench below ground level where I can get a clear view of the parking lot before I walk up the stairs. I don't want to get caught by someone. Abe Lincoln and a skeleton exiting a locked building would only arouse attention.

It was a lush time of year, the plants were

blossoming, the birds were waking at 4 A.M.

This morning I surprised someone near the handrail. It was an orange dog just outside the door in the threshold where a doorman would stand in the days of grand hotels. "Hello there," I said. I've seen deer on the other side of the paving, squirrels of course, lots of birds, but never a dog. This one let me scratch her neck.

Lucky, who had been chatting away moments ago, had become quiet.

I noticed that. "You okay?" I asked him.

The dog telescoped its eyes.

Lucky said, "I'm not too fond of dogs, you know…They like bones."

I didn't think of that. He wasn't kidding either. He was a dog magnet. The dog stared at Lucky like an empty well.

CHAPTER 10

WHEN
I
was
ABE
LINCOLN

When I was Abe Lincoln, I went to the library every day. A homeless president needs something to look forward to. While I wasn't sure how to improve my situation, being Mr. Lincoln helped. Lincoln has its perks but at the end of the day I'm still trying to sleep on a pallet. After I had my coffee I had my routine…it wasn't what I expected from retirement.

I'm sure I made a scene as one of the library regulars. I know they get all sorts of people off the streets, and I was one of them. I didn't have a library card anymore. How could I? Unless I could prove I was Abraham Lincoln with an

1865 ID. So I'd find a comfortable chair by the window and set my coat and top hat on it, to save my spot while I went to the stacks to get a book. That's why books were invented to drive you into another world. The day I met the kid author, I was in Philip Marlowe's 1938 Plymouth coupe in *The Big Sleep.*

He saw me reading and when I got up after a while, he called me over to his table. He told me, "I've written fifty novels so far."

"Is that so?"

It was. The boy continued, telling me about some of them and the one he was writing now. He gave me a sly look and said, "You can be a ghost in this book," and quickly wrote a note on the manuscript.

"Wait a minute—a ghost? But I'm alive." I knocked on the desk for emphasis.

"You're a ghost."

I could tell he was pleased with himself. "But couldn't I be better than a ghost? Maybe a caped crusader or a kindly philanthropist? One of those heroic types?"

He shook his head no and returned to his work.

He was probably writing what just happened

and moving on to what happens next.

I don't like the idea of being a ghost when you're still alive. The boy was so serious, writing me into a book-reality that put me in some haunted mystery. I'd like to know what that boy saw in me. Or would I? Anyway, it wasn't me he was seeing in the library, it was Abraham Lincoln. Maybe I was alright.

CHAPTER 11

BREAKFAST

Lucky and I hadn't gone much further than Sycamore Street when I smelled pancakes. I was headed for my usual rendezvous with the Monte-Cristo consulate, but I didn't make it there. Suddenly all I wanted was pancakes. There aren't any diners around here, it's a neighborhood, with houses, trees and sidewalks and parked cars. The aroma was intoxicating. Somebody was making pancakes for breakfast, homemade, the best kind of all. "C'mon," I told Lucky. I was beginning to believe in that name. If he could summon pancakes, what else could he do?

I stopped on the corner and turned, testing the air. One of those baying hounds from the state prison would help track the smell—unless it realized I was a wanted fugitive and turned its nose on me and barked me up a tree. That was an odd thought but seeing that dog earlier must have inspired it, the same way the things you see in the day can come back to haunt you in dreams. "Can you smell pancakes?" I asked Lucky.

"Does it look like I have a nose?"

"No, but you do pretty good without one, or eyes or ears."

Lucky smiled.

I was bedeviled. "Where's it coming from?"

He pointed a slender arm at the tall hedge surrounding a brick house.

I don't know if Lucky had pancake-radar or what, but he was right on target. I was famished, I scurried like Seymour in a maze. When you live the way I do, you start to lose your sense of... etiquette? Is that the right word? I'm so far from that now. How can a word compare to a reality soaked in syrup and butter? Coffee poured from a silver percolator. I was already through the wooden gate when Lucky asked me what I thought

I was doing.

"I'm going to ask for some breakfast."

"You can't barge up to their door!"

It was too late—I was already there.

"Howard!" Lucky hissed. "You're making a mistake."

I turned my top-hatted head around, "I'm Abraham Lincoln," I said, "I'm starving," and I knocked.

At the base of the steps, Lucky leaned into the rhododendron. The leaves and purple flowers ran through his bones. He was good as gone.

I knocked again and in a moment the door swung open and a woman holding a spatula caught her breath.

"Mr. President!" she gasped.

"Good morning, madam," I nodded. I spoke regally, "I couldn't ignore the enchantment of your culinary talents. By that I mean your pancakes. I set aside all my other morning affairs and made this destination my utmost importance."

"Oh," she said, "Would you care for some flapjacks?"

"Nothing would please me more," I smiled, or rather Abe Lincoln did, a ghost who had traveled a couple centuries to her door.

CHAPTER 12

A
FOREST
in the
CITY

The flapjacks were wonderful, but they did come at a price.

When I was full, Mrs. Fosbury ushered me through the kitchen, out the door to the backyard.

This was no ordinary backyard view of town. No fence, garden, pond or quaint fountain, no swing-set or clothesline, no car parked on dandelions. Penned in between two ten-foot walls on either side, I faced a thick forest. I don't mean blackberry bushes tangled with alders. I was looking at a herd of old growth cedars that blocked out the sky. Each one was wide as an elephant. I couldn't tell how far back they stretched, maybe all the way to Oregon.

"I need you to cut them down," the woman told me. "There's an axe over there against the first tree."

I was speechless. I figured I was going to repay her hospitality by refilling the bird feeder or raking leaves.

"Go on," she gave me a nudge down the first wooden step, "An old Kentucky farmer like you ought to have no trouble. Just stack them like log cabins as you go." She gave me a laugh that flapped after her, leaving me to my job.

Being at school for so long, I can be pulled into thinking it's all about tests, measuring my life that way, and I think I do, to a degree. We're set here like astronauts for a little while. We are here to discover what we can and we try to live good lives. I'm just one drop in the milky way galaxy like everyone else. I'm not going to call my life a miracle—even if it is—because there are times it doesn't feel that way. There are times you get sunk so deep into your own problems you forget to notice the good. These days all I have is Abe Lincoln. I might be reluctant to give up this disguise. I'm not sure how I'm going to go back to being me or if I even want to.

Mrs. Fosbury changed my mind in that regard.

She was as good a reason as any to rethink my life as Abraham Lincoln.

And where was Lucky Skeleton, my lucky charm? Nowhere in sight.

I left the steps and walked toward the woods. I was walking into their radio waves. I could hear birds and far, far in the distance what sounded like a wolf. I stopped when I got to the axe. It was morning, but looking into the endless deep forest it was still cool and dark as night.

I didn't bother with the axe. I was too interested in the trees.

It reminded me of a museum where you enter a dark room that is only lit by the television glow of big landscape windows—Northwest Coast, Southwest Desert, Great Lakes, Eastern Woodlands—with animals frozen inside each scene.

I walked in Witch Woods wanting to notice everything. A red squirrel watched me. An ethereal varied thrush sounded somewhere in the depth ahead. Petrichor. There was no path to follow.

I wouldn't say I got lost. I was past lost. I felt I had time-traveled back a thousand years. I've lived here all my life and never knew there was a forest in the city. My shoes sunk into the green velvet moss and left footprints. When I felt like returning, I could retrace my steps.

I veered around a snail big as a lightbulb.

This was a whole other land.

I don't know how long I walked in it.

"Hey!" someone called me. "How! Over here! What are you doing?"

I laughed. Off to my right, Lucky looked like a puppet atop Fosbury's brick wall. I told Humpty Dumpty's skeleton, "I'm supposed to be chopping down these trees."

"You fool, don't you know anything about fairytales?"

"What?"

"Look around you. It's the world you're living in."

I agreed. "I'm not going to chop it down though."

"You'll be in there until you do," he grinned.

"Forget it."

"Okay," Lucky said, "I'm glad to hear that. Hang on, I'll throw a ladder over for you."

He disappeared, then over it came. The white

bones rattled on the bricks. It was obvious the ladder was made from a skeleton. "Hurry up!" he called from the other side of the wall.

CHAPTER 13

MARMALADE

I had to jump the last couple feet to the ground and all the bones clattered after me. It only took a second for the jumble to become Lucky again. He hopped to his feet.

"I don't know how you did that," I said. I also couldn't believe where I landed, on the sidewalk next to the tall hedge. Behind it was the Fosbury house, hiding the backyard forest. I was thick in the trees a minute ago and now they were gone, replaced by this ordinary city. I didn't expect Lucky to say it was magic and he didn't.

Fairytales.

Does it sound like I'd fall for fairytales? I'm

not the sort to bring a cow to town and trade it for magic beans. I don't believe a cow jumped over the moon either. I don't know how that got started. Who wants to go to the moon anyway? There's no air. But if such a cow existed, it would be a useful getaway. It doesn't even have to be the moon. I'd settle for Mount Shasta. That's far enough. But I don't have a cow, nuzzling flowers in some alleyway.

I didn't have any answers, I just had to be content being here.

As we started to walk again, I was sore, I felt like I already walked five miles. Maybe I did. Who knows how far you can walk in a magic forest? Sometimes my right leg will pain me. It's one of those aging things I can picture leading to a cane in a few years more. That sounds pretty sad, doesn't it? Anyway, who wants to see Abe Lincoln limping on cement?

Not the round glassy eyes of a school bus approaching from behind us. Like a yellow whale it beached next to the curb and sighed loudly. I glanced at Lucky. His expression hadn't changed.

Like a flipper, the bus door waved open and the driver called, "Where you headed?"

The driver chewed an unlit cigar and stared at me, but I let Lucky do the talking. He said, "We're going downtown."

"Yeah? I'm headed that way, back to the bus barn. I'll give you a lift, Mr. President. You and your friend."

Funny isn't it, the way things happen.

If I had followed my usual routine and gone to the Consulat de Monte-Cristo instead, none of this would have happened. I would have had the same continental breakfast I always do. Marmalade toast and a cup of strong coffee. An entirely different reality would have unfolded.

I went up the steep bus stairs, using the smooth handrail to pull myself. I've seen kids bound up and down those stairs. My bounding days were done...at least on this planet...maybe on the moon I'd be able to. The Sea of Tranquility would be my trampoline.

We sat on the first bench seat, me by the window and Lucky hardly taking any room at all next to me. The big yellow door flapped closed taking Abe Lincoln and a skeleton off the curb of Sycamore Street.

"Where you fellahs going to?" the driver asked.

"Louie's Bet Shop," Lucky replied, "Down on Bay Street."

"Yeah," the driver said. "I know where it is."

I let them do the talking. I turned their voices down to a murmur that meshed with the engine and I looked out the window. I was tired from all that walking and South Hill glided by. Way back when, I used to ride a school bus like this. I wondered about the kids who rode it now and if I was fourteen again would I fit in? I doubt it. I didn't then. I recalled my terrible impression of Alfred Hitchcock spinning some story from the telephone wires and the picket fence of a house frozen in tall grass and weeds where something awful had taken place. Gradually the kids would be gone, the bus would empty out. I would hold onto my books and wait for my house. Most of the time I just stared out the window at everything in 1980 set in motion like a stream.

CHAPTER 14

INFINITE WISDOM

The bus stopped on the corner of Holly where it was close enough to walk to Louie's dive, but not so near that it would look suspicious for a school bus in this part of town. By that time the driver and Lucky seemed like old friends, while I was just the man on the penny, along for the ride.

We watched the bus pull away into traffic and I didn't know what would happen next. We were going somewhere I'd never been and somehow it was supposed to land us on solid ground again. I imagine Mr. Lincoln was no stranger to these feelings. When you wear a disguise, you can't help but become a little like that person.

The shadow of The Leopold made an ocean for us to walk across. The sun would climb up its nine-story sides and shine directly down and eventually slide into the sea on the other side. I can still imagine the hotel's coffee shop, a long wooden counter to sit at, booths with soft red upholstery, white tablecloths with candles, dressed in the simple worn elegance of an old couple driving a Mercury sedan.

After Chestnut Street, it was parking lots on your right and left, over the railway bridge, the coppery weeds, metal fences with barbed wire crowns, then down Laurel Street, a cement flatland where the paper mill used to churn. So many places haunt me this way, knowing what used to be here, and now is gone.

We turned the corner onto Granary Avenue and it was as if all the shade had been drawn off the Leopold like a vampire's cape and thrown over this street. Louie's neon sign burned red. Other buildings slouched in the dim around it.

I was tiring again. I was glad to see an end in sight.

Lucky explained his plan while we got closer. It was a crazy. I told him it would never work, it would just make things worse, I'd be in twice the trouble, I wanted nothing to do with it. I stopped at the curb and refused to cross. He promised me it was airtight. He tried to persuade me and make it sound like the musings of an utterly rational mind. Sure...I nodded...Sure...Why not? I took a step. What did I have to lose?

And anyway, who was I to decide whether something was rational. The only way I could face the planet was as Abraham Lincoln.

A motorcycle blatted in the road. Louie's Bet Shop, here we come.

You're not going to believe what Lucky Skeleton in his infinite wisdom decided upon. Go ahead and guess. Then turn the page and be surprised.

CHAPTER
15

NOTHING

"Let me get this straight," Louie said. He clasped his hands together. A burning cigarette stuck from them like a chimney. "You want me to forge a receipt."

Lucky shrugged and nodded, "Not exactly..."

"Really? You telling me you *don't* want me to run a betting slip for Newel Jesper?"

I hushed him and could tell right away from his reaction that he didn't like people doing that. My mistake.

Lucky held up a hand, "Okay, Louie. You're right. That's what we're here for. Only we don't want anyone to know. And remember—you owe me." He grinned, "This will make us even."

A cigarette cloud hid Louie's face. When the smoke cleared, he glared like a pumpkin. Louie thought the offer over and he didn't like it, but he agreed. "Wait here," he said. He got up and left the table. At the end of a long counter was a door.

The TV in the corner showed a horse race. They were bunched together going around the curve. A pinball game chattered and blinked. At the counter a man was playing cards with a robot. The robot had taken a lot of punishment over the years. Laid off from steady work on the mill assembly line, this is where it washed up. Louie's Bet Shop. I wasn't a fan of this place, but so far it looked like Lucky's plan was working.

"What did I tell you?" Lucky grinned.

What a plan...Newel Jesper was the gladhanding vice president of the college. You would see him everywhere. He made it his business to stalk around campus greeting everyone. When Coach Wooden was fired, Newel was the one who made sure the school rehired his best friend. *The Bugle* ran their photo on the front-page.

"I hope this works," I said.

"It's certain to."

I watched the horses blot around the track.

The card game plodded along.

Lucky was humming to the jukebox. I didn't know the lyrics either, but I knew the song. How long would Louie take? A place like this probably has an entire operation, a backroom where counterfeit money flowed off a printing press. The horses were still running. A couple of them were edging ahead. I figured it would be a while sitting here waiting for Louie. I watched the robot draw another card.

Then the door opened and Louie returned. His silk patterned shirt caught the neon and fluorescent lights of the room and made him a firefly. He sat heavily where he was before and the cigarette trembled on his lip, "This makes us even, Skeleton."

"That's right," Lucky smiled.

It was plain to me that Louie and Lucky had been down this road. They knew every crooked shadow and peril while I stumbled on the first basketball.

Louie held an envelope. He held it a moment longer to explain, "I don't want to see you or your fancy pal in here again."

Lucky shook his head.

"And if anything goes sideways," Louie continued, "I don't know nothing."

CHAPTER 16

DREAM ANIMALS

Granary Ave was a welcome sight. Even if it looked like it had tumbled from an ashtray and tried to raise itself with leaning telephone poles, broken glass and neon signs that flickered in the darkness of day, I saw it in a new light.

The incriminating envelope was stuffed in my suitcoat pocket. A skeleton can't carry anything without it being seen. We headed up Chestnut Street. This next part of Lucky's plan was a few blocks away, a six-story white terra-cotta tower with ten-foot blood-red letters on the rooftop. It was a landmark building, a hive that a hundred years of newspapers had flown from, dispersed every day all over the county.

"Just you wait," Lucky promised me, pleased with himself. He had seen the future. It was going my way.

Chestnut is no easy hike. It was getting steeper every step. I could have used Lucky as a walking stick. That last bit up to State Street did me in. Lucky was excited, hopping from foot to foot, we were there, but I had to rest. Lincoln was 56 when he was felled, I'm a little older, but the 19th century was a creaky time, aging its citizens with the weight of all that timber and iron in the coalfired air. I reckon Abe would have removed his stovepipe hat like me to sit on the slatted bench to catch his wearied breath. I watched cars rush by, each one a ghost as soon as it was gone.

Lucky drummed his fingers on the back of the bench. He sighed. I don't know where that breath was coming from, he didn't have lungs, not that I could see—he didn't have eyes either for that matter. Honestly, his entire sentient existence didn't seem possible, but who was I to question? He was right next to me, sighing again, tapping, tapping, tapping.

I stretched my legs out long towards the curbing. My pockets were empty—except for the letter, I didn't need anything anymore—so why was I risking what little I had? Isn't that how my troubles began? Finally the drum solo couldn't be ignored anymore. If it wasn't for that rat-tat-tat, I could have taken a nap. Some people can get away with sleeping on the street, but not Abraham Lincoln, not today. I told Lucky I was ready. I just had to stand back up.

Before I could venture, something startled me. It was either a pigeon or a crab, I can't be sure, I only saw it for a second, flickered at the edge of my sight and gone. Was it hiding under the newspaper vending machine?

I've been seeing creatures like these more often. I have an idea what they are. I think they have something to do with dreams. I've been so tired these days, all I want to do is lie down and sleep, if someone will let me do so without any worry. I think the creatures are here to help, sent from the dreamworld, coming here to take me there. At first just glimpses, in the corner of my eye, scratches, bubbles, shadows, they're taking form, strange animals, getting closer and more daring. They'll get me sooner or later. They know I need to sleep. I think part of me is willing to go with them. Eventually I'll be led away by a couple polka-dot bears or a green giraffe when my time awake is over.

I put a hand on the bench armrest. I'm ready for *The Herald*, I guess.

CHAPTER 17

BURNT COFFEE

The lobby was a checkerboard of black and white marble tiles that played around a metal castle-like contraption. It was an ornate, spired printing press, a gothic anchor sunk deep in a faraway time, when it made dreams that were only shadows now. Black iron frame, waffle platen, gold lettering and trim, with a long thick wooden lever like a harpoon that made me think of the Herman Melville age. I read the notice beside it, "This is a Washington Hand Press manufactured in 1884. The Herald began daily publication on this in 1890."

Lucky wasn't interested. He scratched a fingertip along a framed directory. "That's ancient history," he said, "We're here to *make* history. Come on." He crossed to the wall and pressed the elevator button.

It was hard to stand in the lobby and not imagine all the people who used to rush back and forth, the electricity that ran this place when there were wars and disasters and elections to cover. Nobody ran to the elevator now with a handful of urgent telegraphs. Abraham Lincoln and a skeleton were alone in the lobby. Put that on Page 1.

The elevator door opened and Lucky leaped in. "You still have the envelope?"

I said, "Naturally I still have it."

He pressed the 3 button and held out his bony hand, "Let me have it, I can carry it now."

While the elevator began to rise, he opened the envelope and got the receipt. His grin turned to laughter. "It's all here...Newel Jesper bet $1000 on Washburn University to win, 9 to 1 odds. Final score 114-58. Payoff $20,000!" He laughed again, "Louie did good work."

Above the door, I saw the 3 on the floor indicator panel glow. The elevator stopped. We were there.

The door opened to the saddest looking fake

wood paneling on the wall opposite us. A couple strips unpeeled down banana-style. Lucky hopped out of the elevator, he didn't mind, maybe he doesn't have the sight I do. He doesn't have eyes. Whatever he sees is his own business.

I followed him from the elevator onto the worn brown carpet. The suspended ceiling lights weakly shined and gave the place the look of an Egyptian pyramid chamber. There were other clues *The Herald* had seen better days. Yellowed newspapers were framed in crooked rows on the unsteady walls, historic events, Lindberg landing in Paris, strikes and riots, JFK, the Moon landing.

"Over there," said Lucky. A section of the wall had been cut away to make an open window view of the newsroom beyond. It had a counter to rest your arms on. A suggestion box, a silver bell. Lucky peered through and called, "Hello?"

We couldn't see anyone, just desks and chairs and a slight fog in the air. The mummy smell of the hallway had turned to a sharp burnt odor.

"Is anyone here?" Lucky called.

"Is something burning?" I said.

Lucky dropped a metacarpus on the bell and clanked it a few times.

One of the overhead lights stuttered.

Lucky said, "Where is everyone?"

"I don't know…" The place looked abandoned. There was dust on the suggestion box lid.

"Only ghosts," he said.

"Ghosts that drink coffee," I said. I pointed at the source of that charcoal smell. An empty Sylex coffee pot smoldered like a small campfire amid the husk-like paper leaves on the corner of a desk. "Somebody made coffee and forgot to turn it off." I took a step back and looked for a door. How were you supposed to get in there? Down another hall?

"Give us a leg up," Lucky said, raising a femur.

I made a cradle of my hands and he stepped in, pushed off light as a bindle, and he hopped over the counter. I watched Lucky walk across the old newsroom, past Cary Grant and Rosalind Russell and the bustle that turned to dust.

I said, "Just turn it off so the whole place doesn't burn down. Press that orange button." Funny how even now, in the midst of desolation, that coffee machine continued to run, like a pumpjack on the prairie. We cursed office workers gulp black cups of it, we sup cup after cup like vampires.

Lucky lifted a phalange, pushed the switch and suddenly all the lights in the room went out.

CHAPTER 18

CATCHING SUNLIGHT

I didn't want to admit there was a flaw in his plan, but clearly this scenario was unexpected. *The Herald* was not the beacon of communication it once was. Nowadays when people want the news, they ask a robot.

Lucky was quiet on the short elevator ride to earth. I was quiet too.

Preposterous to think people would think a forged note like that was real. As if the administrator of a prestigious school would feel the need to stoop to my level of criminality. And what was the result supposed to be? Were readers to believe that I could be forgiven if Newel Jesper was also caught profiting from the team? Did that make it right? So what if someone does wrong, look who else does. It goes all the way to the top. We're all corrupt. Is that what Lucky was trying to get across? Honestly, I was glad the newspaper wouldn't be printing the story.

Why start spreading lies?

I could stay Abraham Lincoln a while longer.

When we reached the ground floor and walked onto the chessboard, Lucky stopped on those marble tiles, paused in thought. Then, "Bingo!" he yelped.

"What is it?"

His empty eyes stared at me as he smiled, "I've got it!"

"What?"

He shook his skull, "We don't need *The Herald*. Come on, we're going back to campus."

Up a busy Chestnut Street, past Forest and Garden, we took a right into an alley before we got to High Street. It led most of the long way to the school, plenty of time for us to talk, but Lucky wasn't divulging his new plan. If I had known, I would have used that twenty-minute climb to do my best to dissuade him. The white spire of the

Karate Church was in sight and I was still under the impression that Lucky Skeleton was the brains of this operation.

Brains...that skull was empty as rubber ball.

And yet...I followed him.

We passed a tall hedge and crossed East Maple. The concrete alley was cracked and tarred with seams. Over us ran a path of electric wires sewn to telephone poles. Garbage cans, the backs of houses, chimneys, rooftops scaled with dragon scales. Between the houses, the bay, the distant blue-green shores of the reservation. A plot full of blackberry overgrowth. Laurel Park was coming up on the left.

At first I wondered if it was a mirage—was I that tired that I was seeing things? I stopped.

A signpost was planted in the cement. It looked like an everyday city sight, one of the hundreds of signposts that stand on corners directing traffic, but this was an odd place for it to be, at the start of an overgrown footpath, and unlike those other well-traveled streets and roads and avenues, the name on this sign read: Witch Woods.

"That's strange," I said, "I don't remember seeing that before." As Abe Lincoln, and as myself going back and forth to work for years, I've seen this alley a thousand times and there's never been a signpost pointed into the brush.

Lucky explained, "That's the wood you got lost in. Now that you've been there, you can see the sign, the way is open to you."

"I'm not going back in there," I said. "Not a chance."

Lucky shrugged his clavicles.

It wasn't much further to campus. I could see the brick tower of a residence hall leaning elbows on the leaves. Catching sunlight, the windows shined eyes. In my Abe Lincoln disguise, I thought of the knight Don Quixote. He had the same trouble with windmills coming alive.

CHAPTER
19

CHANDU
the
MAGICIAN

"Stop the press!" Lucky shouted. The newsroom of *The Bugle* was what we wanted *The Herald* to be, a space filled with life. Everyone looked at us. Lucky waved the envelope triumphantly.

A girl left a buzzing teletype and approached. I was used to Abraham Lincoln and a skeleton— the look on her face revealed she wasn't.

Lucky tapped the envelope and asked her, "Are you ready for this?" His bony fingers scrabbled with the flap and he removed the betting slip with a flourish.

She bravely took the paper from his twenty-seven hand bones. I watched her eyes as she read it.

Lucky couldn't stand the suspense, "It's a betting ticket! See the name on it? Newel Jesper! This goes way beyond Howard Harvard. He's nothing, he's only a grain of sand. Vice President Jesper bet against his own institution. And look at the payoff, it's right there on the slip—he pocketed twenty grand!"

By now we had gathered a *Bugle* crowd. Boys and girls read over her shoulder. "We can't run this." She folded the ticket and returned it to the skeleton hand. "Even if it's true, Mr. Jesper is beyond reproach."

"What are you talking about?" Lucky persisted, "This is Pulitzer material!"

The girl glared at me, "Abraham Lincoln...We expected more from you." There was a rumble of assenting voices behind her. Then she smiled and all was forgiven, "The real story is what's a skeleton doing in my office? Tell me about yourself."

"Oh," Lucky grinned. "Now *there's* a story!"

I couldn't believe it. It's odd I never thought to ask him his story too, but, well, we had things to do. He said he was here to help me, I didn't need to question Lucky, I'm not a journalist. But as I faded into the background, I listened to him the way people used to sit around the radio at night, to be entranced by Chandu the Magician. I couldn't believe what I heard.

His story began with a circus in Transylvania. How's that for a start? Do you think the Newel Jesper scoop stood half a chance? The cold wind of a Carpathian night blew the scandal further and further from the front-page. I tugged at the beard spirit gummed to my chin. It wouldn't be coming off any time soon.

Lucky was locked in a steamer trunk, put on a train, rolled over cobblestones, unloaded onto a foreign shore, shipped out once more, torpedoed at sea, floated to land at the end of the Atlantic. America was only the beginning.

When the crowd finally cleared back to their cubicles and desks, typewriters clacking, I told Lucky, "You certainly stopped the press with that story."

"Yes," he grinned.

"Not what I was expecting though. Doesn't exactly get me off the hook, does it?"

His cervical vertebrae wilted, "Sorry. I don't know what happened. It's been so long since I've been in the limelight. I got carried away."

"Yeah…" I agreed. "Now what do we do?"

If he had sleeves to roll up, maybe there would be a winning card.

CHAPTER 20

The
GRAND
SCHEME
of
THINGS

It never crossed my mind to bet on the teams. There's a limit to my villainy. That's commendable, right? It turns out I could've made a killing at Louie's Bet Shop, but I didn't, proving I'm not a racketeer at heart.

I hope that means something.

In the grand scheme of things.

I sipped my free coffee and stared out the window. I was waiting for Lucky. With no more newspapers in town—unless he wants to try *The Shopper's Gazette*—he took his phony betting slip to the President's office in Old Main. I wished him luck. If the story fails to compel them, he can finally drop it. It never seemed like a good plan to me anyway.

It would be simpler if I turned myself in and got this over with. I expect there's someone in the police department assigned to find me and they're running out of ideas—all they want is resolution. Their office desk is piled with dead ends. I'd be doing them a favor if I went to the station. No more outlaw life on the lam. I'm not Robin Hood. I'm not robbing the rich to give to the poor. If anything, they're giving me free coffee, like the one the waitress brought me.

Sofia's Automat is Abraham Lincoln's patron saint. I don't push my luck, but once a day they give me a free coffee. And believe me, I appreciate it. I'm well-aware I only get this star treatment when I'm Abraham Lincoln in the day. Once the moon starts to glow, I turn into Lon Chaney.

As soon as I break this curse and become my old self, I don't think Howard Harvard will ever be forgiven. People will cross to the other side of the street to avoid me. My morning *Herald* will arrive with the crossword done. My takeout dinner will be stone-cold, the bus will ignore me on the road…and worse. When it comes to their sports, people are barbaric. I fully expect to be hunted down. Coach Wooden has made it plain he wants my head stuck like a moose on the wall by the backboard.

Did I actually think I could get away with my scheme? Does every criminal make that mistake? There wouldn't be crime if you knew you would get caught. There must be some doubt. You need to believe you have a chance. There has to be hope.

I sipped my coffee and watched the day turn to dusk.

Lucky was probably in security custody. A mugshot and fingerprints. Another Lucky Skeleton newsbreaking story in the making. The fiend...

"A refill, Mr. President?"

I stirred from the window. "Yes please." I offered her my cup and the waitress complied.

I smiled but I felt bad. I wished I could leave her a tip. I think I have 38 cents in my pocket. Hardly meaningful. It wouldn't help pay her rent. I set the coffee on the other side of the newspaper. The classified ads took up three pages. I went through them every morning looking for something like:

WANTED. Address painter. Pay good. Contact Lex. Worldwide Industries.

Maybe it was time for Abe Lincoln to get a new job.

CHAPTER 21

The
SET
to
POP
PARKING
LOT

Before I became Abe Lincoln, I ran all the numbers for retirement. After all the taxes, bills and mortgage, my take-home pay will be $160. That's not a lot. I needed a part-time job, a few days a week, just enough. The school has jobs like that they dish out on a temporary basis. I figured that would be good and I signed on for one.

There I was, no training at all in delivering babies, working with a teenager who was nine months pregnant. Every morning she was closer. "I'm set to pop," she kept telling me. It made me a little worried. "Look..." I finally said. A cold wind from the sea blew between all the cars as we walked around, inspecting them for parking stickers. Pink cherry blossoms rushed off the tree across the paving. "I'd really appreciate it if you didn't pop when I'm around." I was exhausted with the worry—it was actually keeping me up at night. I even had a book from the library, but I never got past the first chapter. I told her honestly, from the heart, "There's just no certainty I'd be able to help you. Don't expect any heroics. I know it sounds heartless but if you pop, I'm sorry, there's no guarantee." She laughed at me and pulled her sweater over her round swollen shape. A red balloon floated up, tied by a string to her navel. She held it softly between her palms and she showed me, inside, moving, suspended in the fluid, a little child was sleeping. "This is my baby. And when I'm ready—" she held a pin next to the balloon, "I will pop."

I didn't find out if it happened that way or not. I had my basketball Gettysburg instead. The next week I applied for work as Abe Lincoln. They had me fill out a form and I signed it as the 16th president. Previous experience: The White House, legislator, and lawyer in Illinois. Admittedly, I sounded overqualified. My job was painting house numbers. I followed 32nd Street and knocked at each house. Then I would explain how much safer they'd be with their address plainly displayed on the curb for emergency vehicles and delivery vans to see. A donation of twenty dollars was all I requested. I gave a discount to a widow at 819. At the end of 32nd where it met Fielding Avenue, I had $47. I carried my money pouch and receipts to a blue station wagon parked in the lot of Bonita Apartments. Lex was sitting behind the wheel, smoking a cigarette, listening to someone talking on the radio. "What did you get?" he asked me and reached out an arm. I gave him the clipboard and the money. I told him what I made and he went through the receipts and asked, "Is this everything?" I said, "Yes." I wasn't going to lie, I'm Abraham Lincoln. While he counted my nine-dollar commission, I looked away. I was distracted by something I thought I saw, running just over the ridge of Birnam Wood. I searched the sky for a red balloon.

CHAPTER 22

FORGIVEN

The bell on the automat door rang again. I looked up. It was Lucky Skeleton. He was back without the envelope. He spotted me and hurried over to my booth.

Lucky scooted in opposite me and scanned the automat before he spoke. "We're good." His grin seemed wider. "He bought it."

"What?"

Lucky crooked his humerus and shook his hand to silence me. "Shhhhh!"

"Sorry."

With his other hand he took hold of my coffee cup. "Mind if I have a sip?"

"Go right ahead."

"I think I earned it." Lucky took a sip of the black coffee, his cup of outer space.

I don't know where the coffee went. It disappeared past his mandible.

He said thanks and, "Get this, How…You're not going to believe this."

I said, "Wait—they let you see the president?"

If he had eyes, they rolled. "What a scene. Right off, the secretary dives under her desk when I walk in. So I made my own way to his office. I showed him the betting slip and he wasn't surprised, turns out he knows this is happening. It's no secret. That place is filled with secrets. They're all betting like mad around there, it's worse than Vegas." Lucky took a break and reached for more coffee. Gulp. Unnerving. Then he began again, "He assumed I was there to shake him down. He asked what I wanted to keep this quiet. I said you need to pardon Howard Harvard. I told him How's learned his lesson. Just make up a reason and tell everyone a mistake was made. Mum's the word. I promised you could forget what you know. And then…." He leaned over the formica, "Listen how I got them to sweeten the deal. They're giving you a top floor room in the Alumni House, gratis, a beautiful room with a view of the bay. You're set!" Lucky leaned back against the red vinyl bench and grinned.

He was right: I couldn't believe it. "I'm forgiven?"

"Certainly! The president knows someone who works at *The Herald*. You'll be front-page tomorrow morning. Exonerated!" He spread his hands in the air like a headline in bold.

"*The Herald?* Did you tell him their building is deserted."

"Apparently they moved. They have an office in a shopping plaza now."

I stared at my drained coffee cup. "My troubles are over?"

"Naturally! You've got nothing to worry about. It was all a tragic misunderstanding. They're letting you off the hook! And don't forget, that's not all..." he raised my cup in an empty salute, "You're done with Old Main. You couldn't ask for a better ending."

That's true...but I got the feeling we weren't at the ending yet.

"This is your last night sleeping in the attic," he

laughed. He set the coffee cup down. He was still laughing as the waitress reappeared.

"More coffee, Mr. President?"

"Oh no," I put my hand over the cup, "I'm fine."

Lucky seemed surprised that Abraham Lincoln was getting more attention than a walking, talking skeleton. To me, it's just show biz—I'm the one wearing the top hat and the charcoal suit. Also, I'm already a star, people recognize me. Besides, half of Lucky is air. You can see right through him.

Lucky cleared his throat. I glanced at him. I reconsidered and asked the waitress, "Well, maybe just one more refill, please."

I left Lucky to enjoy that cup of night. I told him I wanted to walk to the Alumni House. Before it was dark, I wanted to see my new home. "I'll see you later then." We are stitched to the seasons. We go round and round like yarn. I have made it through the cold days, now I look forward to a hammock strung between two green trees.

Sofia's was starting to fill with the dinner crowd. The glass wall was stocked with sandwiches, stew, salads, and desserts on plates. I wasn't hungry.

Those fairytale pancakes were still keeping me going. I left down the cement steps. The tall poplars whispered. I didn't have far to go. I would be living on the edge of campus. The setting sunlight made the bricks purple. The path took me along rhododendrons and ferns and a pocket of cedar trees, past the copper Bird Sanctuary plaque, put there in 1921.

Lucky could tell me what the evening robins were saying. I didn't need to ask for an exact translation—I know they're happy. A long day is over, they are going to sleep soon. With nightfall, the security guard would be walking the halls in Old Main, turning off lights and locking doors. Once that white pickup truck retreated, I could sneak in for the last time.

Some girls walked by and said hello and their laughter trilled. One of the girls had a flower in her hair. It's early summer after all. I tipped my top hat. Would anyone remember Abraham Lincoln once walked along this path? Maybe there will be a plaque in this spot when I'm gone, just a little away from the Bird Sanctuary.

CHAPTER 23

The
MOVIE
with
FAY WRAY

I was reminded of Don Quixote again. That same tall residential hall with two hundred eyes let me pass. It was just a building, not a Spanish windmill giant. I turned downhill on Oak Street, beside the big lawn of the Alumni House and entered the alley on the bayside so I could see where my room will be. There are two big windows on the third floor and a balcony with a blue railing. Tomorrow night I'll be sitting out there watching the sun run to Japan. Tomorrow night I'll be laying down in a bed, under covers, in the quiet. The window will be open, there will be a breeze coming in from the bay. I'll be retired, I'll be making $160 a month, but look where I'll be living, in the clear.

Not bad. Tomorrow gives me something to look forward to.

Funny, I was walking up this same alley this morning and look what a day has done.

It's a miracle. I don't need *The Herald* to tell me.

I started walking down that alley again, past the ivy and set of stairs leading to my new residence. A porchlight ember burned on the balcony.

This was after five o'clock when there were parked cars home from work. Windows were lit with gold, and the cat next door was asleep under a creeping wave of blackberries. It opened its eyes as I passed. I felt like taking a little stroll. I crossed narrow Ivy Street, practically an alley itself, and thought of Laurel and Hardy pushing a piano up that steep incline. It would take them half a reel to get this far. While I pictured that movie, Lincoln's reflection stuck to the window of a car angled against the curb. Tonight that reflection would go back inside a trunk in the attic of Old Main and hopefully never be seen again.

The alley continued to unroll, I was introducing myself to my new neighborhood, getting to know the details. One house had a string of bells tied to the rainspout, a windchime waiting for the wind. I wanted to cut back to High Street, but Ivy was a dead-end and I guess I'd have to go all the way to Myrtle unless I turned around.

That's when I heard the whistle.

It came from behind me, towards school.

The first time I heard that sound I was at the gym getting water.

Another shrill bit the air. Closer, clearer, sharper. There was nothing Mardi Gras about it. I knew the sound—it was a coach's whistle—and I knew who was ringing the alarm. I heard shoes slapping the pavement full tilt as they turned the corner onto Oak. I caught a glimpse of the basketball team before their shadows got lost in silhouettes. I had to get moving.

Have you read *The Most Dangerous Game*, or seen the movie with Fay Wray?

The modern remake would be *Hunting with Coach Wooden*. It would feature shaky camera work, a pack of athletes let loose in front of Coach Wooden while he brayed and whistled into the night and they chased some poor doomed fool like me.

They were getting near. Their giant shadows crept over the corrugated wall of a garage. Another whistle. Now I thought of the crocodile in Peter Pan. It tick-tocked closer and closer.

I'm not used to running, I'm a long way from that ten-year-old me who might have stood a chance getting away. Mercifully, just before I reached Myrtle Street, I saw the sign for Witch Woods.

CHAPTER 24

OTHER
PLANES
of
EXISTENCE

It's nighttime in the forest too. I'm up a tree on a branch with my back to the trunk. I heard a wolf a minute ago. That's why I'm ten feet off the ground. There's no sound of traffic on I-5 or surrounding streets. No city, only trees. How could this much forest be in our city? I'm in the same place, in the same space of time—it could be drawn on a blackboard—we're on a common plane of existence where other realities are overlaid. If that doesn't make sense, there's bound to be a Quantum Science teacher around the school who can explain. Not in these woods though. It's just me and that wolf and a million trees.

I'm going to try and sleep. There's not much else I can do. I've made myself safe on this branch. Never mind the wolf. In the morning I'll climb down and explore. I can try backtracking to where the alley let me in and stranded me.

I yawned like Robin Crusoe. I shut my eyes. Once I let my thoughts settle, I could listen to the woods.

The trees have their own language, like skyscrapers filled with telephones and telegrams talking back and forth. An owl called across the distance.

There's a library upstairs in Science Hall. It's where I go when it rains and I don't take my lunchtime walk on the wooded hill. It's a big creaky wooden room with stuffed birds on display here and there. Trumpeter Swan, Bald Eagle, Red Tailed Hawk, Canadian Goose, Snowy Owl, Great Blue Heron. They look alive, trapped behind glass, as if the cases have vacuum sealed them in and only a breath of our air will get them moving again. I find a seat near one and I listen to them, watch them for the slightest motion. They make me a little distracted. Who could read with a swan curved only inches from you? When it rains and I don't walk on Rome Hill, this is where I go, beside the window and the Great Grey Owl.

An owl called across the distance.

That otherworldly sound took me to the memory of a little bookstore that used to be downtown. I went there every week or so. Don't let a cat slip out when you open the door. One time I found a little Laurel paperback of Emily Dickinson poems there. The woman who owned the store lived on the second floor above it. She told me it was cheaper to live where you work. Money didn't come easy. When I bought my book of poems, she solemnly took my four dollars and filled out a receipt slip in the ornate script of an auction house cataloger. Often, I was the only one in the shop. Business wasn't great. She hired a contractor to put in an espresso machine and a marble counter, thinking to supplement her income with coffee drinks. I thought it was a good idea. She had it for about a week then she stopped using it. She told me why. "The cats don't like the sound."

An owl called across the distance.

Well, I don't mind owls at all. I counted the seconds between its next call...like waiting for thunder after a lightning flash...Thirty-two seconds...I tried to count again but the numbers crumbled. I felt cradled in the tree. The owl reached a black wing over me and I slept until I woke up with the little birds in the pale light of dawn.

CHAPTER 25

WORLD WITHOUT END

I retraced my steps as well as I could. No sign of the alley or Myrtle Street, no sign of tire tracks on the moss or unsnapped twigs…no clue how I dropped into this place. Here's an interesting development though—somewhere along the way I lost my Lincoln top hat, either in the mad race from Coach Wooden's mob, or here in the forest. Also, there was no reason for the fake beard anymore. I peeled it off. Some plucky bird could use it to line its nest. I was practically myself again…whenever Witch Woods was ready to let me return to my modern world.

The ground was uneven, it would dip and

stagger me, covered in mossy waves and ferns with fallen trees and limbs I had to clamber, branches that scratched me and roots that tried to trip me. Way above in the treetops a current pushed and seethed, a breeze like a rushing stream. After a hundred yards, or two hundred, or half a mile, it felt like I was in a world without end. I rested on a stump growing a bright green sail of huckleberry. It was months too early for the red berries. I wondered if I was walking like a ghost through the other plane I was from, the one with Sofia's Automat and the Safeway on Cornwall Avenue. At this very moment in a parallel reality, I might be sitting atop a pyramid of oranges for sale. I could be on campus, standing in the shallow fountain in Red Square, or there might not be students, I might be surrounded by deer. Hundreds of them. I could reach out and brush them as they passed.

This seemed a good place for those strange animals to be, the ones from the dream world, but the only creatures I saw were real—little birds that climbed the rigging of the firs, up and down the bark. Beetles, a black and yellow millipede, a honeybee, a spider's web. The more I stayed still, the more I became part of the forest. Then I saw a deer. It went smooth as silver and silently, no breaking shoots to give it away, while it drifted by and out of sight like a dream.

I see deer quite often as I walk around town. It's magic how they come and go. I don't know how they find home in our fabricated world, how they survive, how they can glide in and out and hide the way they do. Maybe this forest has given me a clue. It seems they use Witch Woods too. You can almost catch them as they leave, across yards and streets, across time, back hundreds of years through this century, the walls we put up, the motorized age, all our noise and confusion, our temporary blur. The deer fade further and further to a place where they know most of us don't remember.

I stood and I could feel how tired I was as I tromped to where the deer had been. The one thing my wandering was lacking was a good path. When I climbed free of the undergrowth, I was standing on a worn deer trail. The deer have been using this like taxi cabs to go from place to place. There was no better route for me to follow.

If anyone knew the way to Myrtle Street, I was sure a deer could lead me back.

CHAPTER 26

LOOKING
for
HOWARD
HARVARD

It was a well-polished path, smoothed by hundreds of deer taxi hooves, I was hopeful I would find it leading to the Leopold Hotel, or Boulevard Park, or whatever other popular spot taxis go. I only seemed to be traveling in more endless forest. If there was a map of Witch Woods, it wasn't posted anywhere I could see.

One thing about being alone, it gives you a lot of time to think.

I sat in the woods on a hill just listening to the light rain and enjoying the peace, when a big creature took shape. It stayed in sight. It resembled a blue mountain gorilla.

I was almost relieved when I saw the gorilla. Finally I had someone to talk to. It didn't matter if this was a dream—I was happy to explain. "I think I'm finally getting it. There are worlds within worlds. You want me to realize that. There are two worlds, anyway, maybe more, why not?" I drew a circle on an imaginary chalkboard. I knew I wasn't in a classroom, but here I was acting that way, making circles in the air. "The dreamworld is here. And next to it is..." another circle, "our reality." I took a step back, looked at the gorilla watching me thoughtfully. Then I returned to the board and erased the two circles. "Now...when I fall asleep..." I drew the dream circle again, then the reality circle overlapping it slightly, "The two worlds meet. And this is where I am right now, here in the middle."

"Hey professor," said a familiar voice. Funny, all it took was two words and I knew who it was. Sure enough, Lucky Skeleton was standing in a doorway cut into the woods. I could see the Leopold behind him. Pigeons in the gray sky. "I had a feeling I'd find you here." A bus went past him. I felt the exhaust. "You ready for breakfast? I could use a coffee."

The gorilla was gone and once I stepped through that frame into the city, so was Witch Woods.

"Watch your step," Lucky warned me. I dropped from the back of a van and landed on the hard street. I turned around, no sign of the forest, I had jumped off a *Herald* delivery truck.

"Hey!" Lucky said, "Grab one of those newspapers, let's see if you're pardoned."

Where there would have been salmonberry a minute ago, I freed a paper from a stack and handed it to him.

Lucky snapped it open and scanned the front-page. "Well…it's not on page one…Aww, tell you what—let's not read it til we get some coffee. Let's go."

I shut the van's door. It would be hard to explain what I was doing in there. It would look like I was stealing newspapers. Actually, that's true, I did. I caught up with Lucky and as I glanced nervously at the Sears display windows passing us, I saw the manikins dressed for summer, and I saw our reflections gliding across that view. My Lincoln disguise was gone. If people are still looking for Howard Harvard, I'm in trouble.

CHAPTER 27

SHOWBOAT

The Imperial Café on East Holly has a slogan: "Good Food." There's a photo of Abraham Lincoln on the brick wall inside. I'm shaking hands with the owner. The waitress, not in the photo, seated Lucky and me at a window with a view of the alley.

"Can I get you started with a coffee?" she asked.

"Two," blurted Lucky. "Two for me. You having any, How?"

"Yes please."

"Three coffees," the waitress said.

Lucky gave a thumbs up and rustled *The Herald* onto the tabletop. "Let's see…"

I could read the headline: *How to Park on a Hill.* Below the bold lettering it continued in smaller print, *Don't rely just on your park brake.* Shame I couldn't top that story.

Lucky loudly turned to the next page. I was afraid to ask...He huffed and turned pages again.

The waitress returned with two coffees she set before Lucky. One cup had a painting of a horse, the other was a sailing ship.

"Oh," he looked up, "Could you bring me a Danish too?"

She nodded and left...to get my coffee I hoped.

Lucky went right ahead and took a loud sip, then back to *The Herald.* He turned more pages.

"Did you miss it, maybe?" I said.

He shook his head. It looked like he was on the last page. "Lost Bird, a macaw named Federica..." He turned the paper over and creased it on the table. He took another sip that turned invisible. "That's good coffee."

The waitress was on the other side of the room, writing a new order.

I said, "I wonder if she forgot about my coffee."

"Ahah!" Lucky yelped. He tapped the square article and read three sentences. It said I was making a movie about the basketball team. The film got leaked before it was done. It wasn't my fault, I never meant to have it seen that way. "How about that?" He grinned. "You're back in the fold!"

There was no time to say anything. The waitress returned.

"Your Danish," she said.

"Terrific!" Lucky grinned.

I held up my hand but she was gone before I could speak. I turned, "Where's my coffee?" I asked Lucky.

He was folding the newspaper. "I'm keeping this. Lucky saves the day!"

"I don't know where my coffee is. Do I need to catch her attention?"

He drank from his second cup and repeated wistfully, "Lucky saves the day."

There was a table between us as I called to the passing waitress, "Excuse me."

She stopped in mid-motion. She grabbed the hand towel off her shoulder as if she needed to clean a spill. Is this what it's like, not being Abe Lincoln?

"Could I get a coffee please."

"Sure."

It was obvious she wouldn't cherish the moment she brought me coffee and sure enough when I read the message painted on the cup I got the point loud and clear. It said: Showboat.

I showed it to Lucky and he laughed, "She got you!"

CHAPTER
28

CRISWELL
PREDICTS

I feel a little strange about the pardon, I mean I really did make that film and send it to other schools, and I really did want to make money off that plot. That seems criminal, but like Lucky found out, they're all doing it here. It's just supposed to be hush hush. They kept it quiet by paying me off.

Lucky finished his pastry and reached for a napkin. "Hey!" he said and tapped a silver contraption mounted to the table, "They have a Criswell Predicts." I've been in diners before that have a table jukebox, maybe eight songs you can punch in for a quarter. A jukebox or predictor was just a way to fill in the time while you waited for your meal.

"You got a dime?" Lucky asked me.

"I'm down to the last of them."

"Don't worry about money." Lucky snapped his fingertips until I gave him ten cents. He inserted the coin and waited for the reply. The machine whirred. An orange strobe blinked. Then a slip of paper appeared.

Lucky got it and read what it said, "I predict that your next savory seasoning will be powdered pineapple, to be used in all cooking, from meats, dressings, puddings, salads and even to sweeten coffee or tea!"

Lucky nodded. "Isn't that the truth. He was right about that." Next to salt and pepper shakers and the ketchup, he retrieved a shaker of yellow crystals. "I used to do a little prognostication myself, back in Transylvania. When you tell someone something extraordinary, saying it makes it real. Maybe only in imagination or dreams, but somewhere it's real. Some of my fortunes were funny, some of them ridiculous, some as awful as Nostradamus—and if they weren't exactly true in this world, at least they were reminders to believe in infinite wonders and possibility." He dashed some pineapple powder into his cup.

I shuddered. I never got used to the taste of pineapple in coffee. I know it's all the rage, it just isn't my cup of tea.

By now, Lucky had opened *The Herald* again. He smiled at the back page and opened the paper, "At least they could have placed our news ahead of the classifieds..." He ruffled the paper. He stopped in the personals section and traced a bony finger along the type. The lonely and lost are always around. Then he gasped as he read aloud, "*Dear Tall, Dark and Lincoln...*What's this?"

"What?" I reached for the newspaper.

He laughed at my reaction. "Oh, How! I'm *joking.*"

Of course he was. But for a second I actually believed. What a buffoon I am. I go to work, then I go home, how could I meet anyone? I'm alone in the universe. Not even America's beloved Abe Lincoln can help me. It's too late I'm afraid. Love is a mystery I've never been able to figure out.

Lucky didn't have any trouble getting refills for both his cups, anytime they were running low, the waitress reappeared, but my Showboat cup grew cold.

I said, "Do you think she's mad at me for being

Howard Harvard?"

Lucky put one hand on the predictor and tapped its chrome shell, "No...she's not mad, she just doesn't care. You're not Lincoln anymore. From now on you're just an ordinary old man."

CHAPTER 29

The
HOWARD
HARVARD
FAN
CLUB

Oh, something unexpected *did* happen as we were getting ready to leave. Lucky was satisfied, he had enough coffee. I had given up on my empty cup, so cold and forgotten and shipwrecked in a frozen sea. I stood up and I was searching my pockets for money. Lincoln's ragged black suit coughed up some coins and crumpled dollars. I hoped it was enough. I was counting it when I sensed someone approaching me. For a second, I thought it might be one of those dream creatures here to knock me out.

"You're Mr. Harvard, right?"

I guessed they were students. He stared at me like someone with flowers for eyes. The girl next to him wore a button that read: **Where's Howard?** I pushed one last quarter from a jumble of copper coins. I said, "Yes."

"I told you!" the girl chirped. Then she said to me, "I knew it was you!"

Some more of their friends quickly gathered around our table. "We're the Howard Harvard Fan Club," the boy said.

"We think you're wonderful," she said.

"You're an inspiration," another boy said.

"Howard Harvard!" someone hoorayed.

They wanted me to say something. It seems like all of a sudden I'm no longer the enemy. They were cheering me. They thought what I did was great, sabotaging the school and diving underground. It was revolutionary. I saw my name on more buttons. When I was young like them, I felt the same way. It's so easy to see the system as something wicked and its foes as heroes. I waved and took a chance.

"Thanks…Thanks for—" Someone whooped. I said, "Thanks for being on my side. I've had a difficult time…nothing happened the way I hoped it would. This cheers me though…Honestly, I didn't know anyone cared. I've never had a fan club before, I'm not sure what you do exactly, but…I appreciate…" A camera flashed. "I appreciate you, thank you. I'm glad you found me, your search is over, you don't have to wonder Where's Howard? anymore. I'll be around. Today is my first day of freedom and I guess I'm ready to see what that's like. Thanks."

The applause that followed swept the café. It was no Lincoln speech—you won't hear future children reciting it for their class. It was a brief moment in time, my fan club can probably go back to their lives. They stepped aside and let me and Lucky break for the door. What an occasion! I gave one last wave before we left. Through all the happy faces, I saw the waitress with her coffee pitcher. She wasn't impressed. I'm sure I'm not the only one this has happened to. Not everyone you meet can love you.

CHAPTER 30

WHERE
the
LINOLEUM
ENDS

We had no need for subterfuge getting into Old Main, the doors were unlocked, it was past 9 AM. People come and spend all day in here. It's their routine. Down our usual hallway, we walked past open office doors. Someone typing would turn into the sound of the next person typing. File cabinets wheezed and clacked. Voices. The iron will of a ticking wall clock. The industrious sounds of a beehive.

I glanced at the locked hatch, but we didn't stop for the crawlspace. That was no longer the way to my room—what used to be my room. We continued down the hall and took the elevator to the fifth floor.

Lucky shook his head and grinned at me, "You've got a fan club now."

"Yeah…Well, I may not be so interesting anymore. I plan on staying out of trouble for good." I meant it too. The next issue of their newsletter *The Howard Harvard Regard* would be me in a hammock, sound asleep. I might share a recipe, or the best way to grow wisteria. I was retired, what did I care? I could do what I wanted, the world was finally mine. If they're disappointed, I'll tell them don't worry, there's always someone else ready to make waves.

The elevator stopped and the door slid aside.

Lucky led the way, but first he turned and put a skeleton finger to where his lips would be and hushed me. A few shut doors lined the hall. We had to be quiet, whoever was banished up here was a long way from the conference rooms and big decisions. The fifth floor needed its own lighthouse to warn you of shadows, papercut reefs and whirlpools that would pull you in. The elevator clanked shut. Shoe soles and bare bony feet were the only sound.

Where the linoleum ends, we stopped at the base of a metal ladder that rose to the ceiling. The attic was after that. Lucky put a hand on a rung and pointed up.

I could see the padlock at the top. "How do we get that trapdoor open?"

Lucky wagged his index phalange and grinned. "You ever hear of a skeleton key?" He demonstrated, twisted his wrist, and turned the finger. Then he ascended, quick as a pirate flag. He rattled the lock for a moment then it unclasped. Hooked against the ladder, he scratched the trapdoor aside.

That sound made me nervously check the hall both ways. No door flew open clattering abacus beads and typewriter ribbon. When I looked back at the ceiling, Lucky was gone into the darkness. I tried to be quiet as I climbed. I didn't know that an unmarked door next to the custodian's closet was open just enough for an eye to be watching.

CHAPTER 31

MOTHS

I wasn't bringing much to my new place. I didn't arrive with much and in my disgrace my old landlord had cleared out my apartment, so I am starting from square one. I had my old clothes on. I folded the charcoal suit and placed it back in the Drama Department locker. I was sorry I lost Lincoln's top hat. If they plan on staging his return, they'll need to find a new one. I hope it shall not perish from the earth. I pictured a deer wearing a spirit gum beard, walking out of Witch Woods with the top hat on its antlers.

I said, "What about you, Lucky? Are you coming to the Alumni House?"

"No. I belong here in the attic. You never know when I'll be in demand again."

"That's true," I said. "You sure helped me." If it wasn't for Lucky Skeleton my life as Abraham Lincoln could still be going on.

"Anyway, I'll walk you there, make sure you get settled in."

"Thanks." I shoved a box onto the pallet where I slept. I wanted to make it look the way it used to. "I guess that's it. I'm done."

"You dragging that shag rug with you?" Lucky meant my blanket.

"Yes." I figured I earned my polar bear skin. I held it bunched to me.

"You bringing those moths with you too?"

One of them danced in front of my eyes. The daylight through the slatted shutter made another pair flicker. I shook the thick fur and there were more. I felt like King Kong on top of New York. I was carrying a moth airport. "Oh!" I groaned, "Let's get out of here!" Would I miss this place? Not at all. As for the moths, they were headed to Vienna Cleaners.

CHAPTER 32

MILLIE

Millie was waiting for me as I reached the bottom of the ladder.

I was surprised. We both got old working here. We started in the same department many moons ago before our hair turned white. My first boss was Edward G. Robinson from The Sea Wolf. Thankyou Human Resources Department for letting that happen. Of all the administrative robots they could choose from the catalog, they settled on Wolf Larsen. He kept everyone in a state of fear, every quarter there would be someone getting fired. Tears were common as faucet water. It was horrible. When you work in an office all day five days a week, it shouldn't feel like a shanghai. We were lucky to have Millie there. She was a kind reminder and funny as Joan Blondell—my God, to hear someone laugh and see someone smile—she was miraculous. She always was.

I can't believe Millie is marooned in Old Main too, they have her hidden on the 5th floor, in an unnumbered room next to a broom closet. I should have looked for her, but time just carried me away. I was caught in a dream as small and large as the Milky Way Galaxy.

I'm discovering the older you get, time keeps playing games. Sometimes I'll see someone I think I used to know, the clothes, or walk, or sound of their voice. Just the same! But how could that be? Surely the person I'm remembering would have grown older. Nobody stays locked in time, only in memory.

"How are you?" she asked.

I said I was fine. I said I was retired. She said she saw an article about me in the paper and I said don't believe everything you read. Pretty soon we were laughing like the old days. I forgot a skeleton was standing next to me.

"What brings you here?" she asked, "Were you

missing me?"

"Of course. It took me years, but I finally found you."

She pointed at the ladder. "Were you looking on the roof?"

I tried to think of an answer, something to do with gargoyles maybe, while I brushed at a moth. This white blanket beast was a snowfield full of moths.

She ducked a pair of wings. "Are you taking your pet for a walk?"

"No…" Another moth fluttered off. "This is an old polar bear who died of stage fright."

"Mmhmm," she said. "And you found that poor creature on the rooftop?"

"Somewhere like that." I wished Lucky would help me out, but he only stood there observing.

Millie crossed her arms, "You know there's talk of a ghost that lives up there in the attic."

"Really?"

"Someone from *The Bugle* asked me about it. They were doing a story. I told them the ghost was just a rumor made up for publicity, to give the old building some character, and anyway, even if it's true, I don't suppose we'll hear much from it anymore. What do you think?"

I don't know how ghosts work, but I was sorry if I was reading into her words, and she meant me. I missed her company, I shouldn't lose sight of her, I don't know what happened to me. I shouldn't have forgotten. I promised her I'd be back again, I promised, but I had to go—by then we were standing in a moth vortex.

CHAPTER
33

IMPOSSIBLE
ANIMALS

We were on the way to Vienna Cleaners, Lucky and me. I was carrying the polar bear, sowing moths in the alley while I went. It wasn't raining anymore. A cool June morning. There was a bird traffic jam on the overhead wires. They sounded like people stuck in cars.

By now Old Main was blocks away. I told myself I would get used to this alley. I would have my favorite trees, cats to say hello to, dogs to pet, I'd know the backyards and broken-down cars, and everyday I'd walk past that Witch Woods sign. I hear bells in the air and not just the birds and the distant roar of cars and a train horn crawling through downtown. The bells are gone now. I know I heard them though. Something was ringing up in the trees. We're never far from mystery, are we? I asked Lucky, "Did you see who I was talking to when you found me in the woods?"

"The blue gorilla?"

I told him how I had been seeing animals like that for a while. All my life. They used to walk into my room at night and shadow the wall. Once I was on a long road trip and I was so tired I could barely keep my eyes open, and in the road ahead of me I saw giant yellow rabbits. They wanted me to join them on the other side of the median, in their eternal fields. Instead, I pulled to the side of the road and slept on the grass near the shoulder. Cars and trucks shot past. When I woke up, I was covered in tiny bug bites. I saw the shadow of a huge bird, but the sky was empty and the shadow was gone. I went back to the car and slept on the back seat. My time awake is limited. They know when my life is on edge, when I just need to rest. They remind me every day. They seem to be getting bolder too. That's what I told Lucky Skeleton. Aren't they here to help me sleep?

Lucky shook his head no. He told me dreams

are their own reality. Whoever lives in a dream can't travel to this world, they can't breathe the air. The creatures I've been noticing are different. "You shouldn't be able to see them yet. They're not really part of this world. They're from another world, the next world, the one you call Death." He let me hold that cold balloon thought for a moment.

"How do you know that?"

Lucky stared at me, jaw slightly open. "Come on," he said, "I'm a talking skeleton. I know about Death. And I know about you. Did you think I just happened to be locked in a casket in Old Main for no reason? I'm keeping an eye on you. If I didn't show up at Witch Woods when I did, you'd be gone."

"Oh jeeze," I said. "Is that why those animals are here, to get me out of here?"

"Yes!"

"Well, what do I do?"

"Try not to notice them. They're after you. The more you notice them, the closer they get, the more they lure, and the weaker you'll be to resist them."

I swatted at a moth. "Okay..." What could I

say?

It made me wonder for the first time exactly who Lucky Skeleton was. I mean, I heard his *Bugle* story, how he got here from Transylvania in a steamer trunk, but what is he doing here? What if he's from Death too? He is a skeleton, after all. That didn't seem right though, he only ever helped me to *stay* in this world. Maybe he's a guardian angel...We walked in silence until the next street corner brought us the sight of someone in a long dark coat and fedora smoking a cigarette.

The man looked so out of place in his 1930s clothes. "Is that another death messenger?" I asked.

"No, that's just a ghost. One you probably know."

I laughed. I did know him. Our town has a history that includes Clark Gable. In 1935 he was here making a winter movie, walking on these very sidewalks, going to cafés and matinees, never leaving apparently.

"He doesn't see us," Lucky told me.

We walked right by him like a pair of impossible animals.

He was intent on that cigarette. It glowed

against him and turned into a puff of smoke.

A moth headed for him. I hoped it was the last of them.

CHAPTER
34

TAKEN
to the
CLEANERS

"I think the moths are all gone, they're all over town now."

The cleaner turned the white fur coat until he found a tag sewn inside. He looked over his glasses at me, with a changed expression just from reading words, "Do you know what this is?"

"Polar bear?"

"Did you neglect to read this?"

"No, I couldn't. I was living in the dark, I didn't have electricity."

He looked at me peculiarly. "Read…"

Another thing I wish I never lost: my glasses. I squinted at the fine print. *"Property of Republic Pictures…White Pongo.* White Pongo?"

"White Pongo was a movie star," the cleaner explained.

"I never heard of him."

"He was in movies back in the forties and fifties."

"Really?"

He took on the air of a professor, "I happen to be a collector of cinema history, the Golden Age, in particular. Did you notice the wall? I have photos of all my favorite stars. White Pongo's up there somewhere..."

We searched the framed photographs windowed along the wall, rows of stars like a flock of rare birds. "There he is—next to Marie Windsor—it's signed too."

White Pongo was a gorilla. I tried to imagine that big ape stopped in a hotel lobby, autographing the photo for a fan, but the cleaner interrupted me, "Where did you get this?" then quickly amending himself, "No—don't tell me! If it's hot I don't want to know." His fingers clutched at the animal skin. "Let me ask you, sir. Would you consider selling this?"

I wasn't planning to. Once it was moth-free I thought it would end up on my new bed although the concept of bed seems foreign to me. Those dark attic nights, when I thought it was a polar bear, it was my companion and only comfort, but I didn't even know what was disguised. A gorilla named White Pongo? If anyone ever went looking for White Pongo in the dark of Old Main, they would have to conclude the moths finally finished him off. They were well on their way.

I regarded the cleaner's attention and his love of the Golden Age, and it only made sense, Vienna Cleaners was the perfect home for White Pongo. I said, "You should keep it." I have all I need.

The cleaner was delighted. "I'll put Pongo in the corner by the door!" I smiled. I could picture the scene some November rainy night when someone on the sidewalk—a screenwriter searching for inspiration—would look in and spot that movie star lit by the streetlights and passing cars. A new story would spring into being, bringing that ape suit back to life—*Son of Pongo*—set on the rooftops, swinging on the neon signs and awnings. "This is such a gift, so unexpected," the drycleaner beamed. Then he noticed Lucky Skeleton, "Does your friend need a vest or a nice suit?"

"No thanks," Lucky replied, "I am what I am."

But the cleaner insisted he wanted to do something, "If you ever have any laundry needs, be sure to let me know. It's complimentary."

I didn't think I ever would. The Alumni House has a washing machine. I don't think I'll ever see the likes of another gorilla again either and if I do, Lucky warned me to look the other way. I've had enough misadventures to last a lifetime.

CHAPTER 35

From
TIME
to
TIME

I expected to see signs of all the moths as we walked up the alley again. I expected to see laundry lines hung with half-eaten sweaters and dresses, shirts with only one sleeve, but wherever the moths chose to live was out of sight. I knew the feeling, having been a sort of moth myself for the winter. I asked Lucky if he'd get restless locked back up in that trunk, waiting to be found. I told him there was plenty he could do here in the world. "You could get a job as a sidekick on *The Count Misfit Show*." Saturday late-night TV, hosting old monster movies, he would fit right in. I knew the Count, I said I could put in a good word.

"How," he replied, "Don't worry about me. My job is being Lucky and spreading that luck around." He laughed. "Besides, we had a good time, I'm tired, I need to recharge my batteries. I could use a few peaceful years in a sarcophagus."

A kid in a backyard saw us and ran to the fence. He put his hands on the pickets and his voice rang out, "Are you a real skeleton?"

Lucky tipped his top hat—when did he get that?—and grinned and said, "I most certainly am." A parade of birds were singing on the slanted telephone wire. "And here with me is your new neighbor, Mr. Harvard. I expect you'll be seeing him from time to time."

We said our hellos and when we said our goodbyes, I turned to Lucky, "Is that Lincoln's hat? Where'd you get that?"

"I took the liberty as we were passing Witch Woods." That crazy smile of his looked good under a top hat. It belonged. You don't see top hats very often and when you do, they make you think of Abraham Lincoln. Now when I see one, I'll recall a certain skeleton instead.

Myrtle Street was behind us, the hillside had turned to a jumble of blackberry and ivy and patched in between the tree leaves I could see my new home.

CHAPTER 36

The GOLDEN GATE BRIDGE

Sure enough, just like I hoped to, we sat on that balcony and looked at the postcard perfect bay. There were some white sails and a crab boat coming back from the islands. Its distant growl was followed by a shifting veil of seagulls. I know why I'm so tired, I've been walking in Witch Woods, the effect lingers.

When we entered the Alumni House, I found a letter waiting for me on the floor. It's on the table next to me now. It's from the Academy of Art University. Lucky read it aloud for me earlier. I was worried what it would be. So many things have gone wrong, what if my easy life was about to crumble again, what if we were bound for the Old Main attic again? It turned out that yes, they had reviewed the video tape I sent them, but they considered it a work of art. They thought I entered it in their documentary contest. They were impressed! An Honorable Mention certificate award was included in the envelope. I also received a couple plane tickets for San Francisco to attend their festival.

What do you know?

This was Lucky's encore.

Every half hour or so an airline jet would descend across the skyline over the water from the south. It would land and another would leave going back. I asked Lucky if he wanted to be on one. California was only two hours away by air. I thought he'd like Frisco. It beats Transylvania. I forgot he was a skeleton and didn't have any picture identification or pockets to put it in. He reminded me about Millie up on the 5th floor.

I was thinking of her. It looked like she was also part of Lucky's plan for me. I raised my voice and called. "What's honorable mention mean anyway?"

The kitchen window was open. Lucky was

inside the house making his famous spaghetti. That's what he called it. The smell of cooking sauce.

"Is that like an A-?" I asked.

Lucky answered, "No, it's not quite an A-. Close...Almost...They liked it, but not enough to win."

"They liked it though."

A pan lid clanked. "Let's just say it was mentioned."

I said, "Okay. I get it." Oregano made a gondola on the breeze. I thought about Millie, it was nice seeing her, but we're talking about San Francisco, not a lunch date at the dining hall. Then I decided to ask her anyway. Why not? I looked at the envelope on the table. Amazing! The Academy of Art University liked my movie—who was I to tell them it wasn't art? And why would I?

I said, "I'm thinking about asking Millie if she wants to see San Francisco."

I don't think Lucky heard me. The water was running in the sink. Anyway, I was still testing the thought, driving it into the fog on the Golden Gate Bridge.

CHAPTER 37

PRETEND

People leave the way they arrive, there are just different doors. And escalators and spring-loaded hatches and funhouse stairs. Lucky said goodbye then off he went to Old Main, to sleep in a sarcophagus. The spaghetti was gone. Don't ask me why a skeleton needs to eat, or how. I washed the dishes and left them to dry. On my way to the balcony, I checked the bookshelf. There was only one book, *The Thousand and One Nights*. I opened it randomly I thought. The story in the book turned out to be about a genie granting wishes.

A genie—of course!—that's what Lucky Skeleton is! It's hard to believe how else all of this happened to me. I finally found the rational explanation—a genie did it. Don't expect a Quantum Scientist to buy it, but I do.

The day was turning into dusk, a few stars were appearing, or more likely planets, or both. The blinking lights of another jet landing, and soon another would be retracing that track in the air. I heard a noise on the lawn. It sounded like a deer, and when I first saw the dim shape of it, I thought it was.

Anyone who has been to a zoo or seen the art on preschool walls or watched a movie like *Pongo and the Lost Safari*, will know what a zebra is. There was a zebra on the lawn. It glowed a low blue like an oil stove flame. It was limping. I don't know how it got hurt, there are plenty of ways. I tossed the book onto the table and rushed inside—not because I was afraid—the kitchen has a red First Aid box on the wall. I noticed it as Lucky was cooking, chopping onions like a thresher. I got bandages and gauze and hurried to the balcony.

The zebra stripes rippled. It seemed to be trying to breathe. It took another painful step. I said, "Wait right there, I'll help." And down the stairs I went. I almost slipped but I caught the rail.

Lucky thing. A bright white streetlight standing in the alley made my shadow lean behind me as I ran across the lawn. "Are you okay?"

I kneeled in the blue phosphorus. I couldn't see what was troubling its leg. My dog used to step on blackberry vines and I'd have to fish out the barb. Then again, sometimes an animal will pretend, like the way a killdeer will hobble away from the direction of its nest in the rocks. My knowledge of zebras or the veterinary sciences is slim at best but here I was, like the Set to Pop Parking Lot attendant I used to be, ready to help anyway I can. If there's anything to be learned from this ordeal, it's to be helpful. Isn't that true? That's part of it anyway.

ONE DROP in the MILKY WAY

Started 3/28/23—6/26/23

Illustration by Aaron Gunderson from *Pie in the Sky*
#83, 1994, an underground, unseen Seattle magazine.

Books by Good Deed Rain

Saint Lemonade, Allen Frost, 2014. Two novels illustrated by the author in the manner of the old Big Little Books.

Playground, Allen Frost, 2014. Poems collected from seven years of chapbooks.

Roosevelt, Allen Frost, 2015. A Pacific Northwest novel set in July, 1942, when a boy and a girl search for a missing elephant. Illustrated throughout by Fred Sodt.

5 Novels, Allen Frost, 2015. Novels written over five years, featuring circus giants, clockwork animals, detectives and time travelers.

The Sylvan Moore Show, Allen Frost, 2015. A short story omnibus of 193 stories written over 30 years.

Town in a Cloud, Allen Frost, 2015. A three-part book of poetry, written during the Bellingham rainy seasons of fall, winter, and spring.

A Flutter of Birds Passing Through Heaven: A Tribute to Robert Sund, 2016. Edited by Allen Frost and Paul Piper. The story of a legendary Ish River poet & artist.

At the Edge of America, Allen Frost, 2016. Two novels in one book blend time travel in a mythical poetic America.

Lake Erie Submarine, Allen Frost, 2016. A two week vacation in Ohio inspired these poems, illustrated by the author.

and Light, Paul Piper, 2016. Poetry written over three years. Illustrated with watercolors by Penny Piper.

The Book of Ticks, Allen Frost, 2017. A giant collection of 8 mysterious adventures featuring Phil Ticks. Illustrated throughout by Aaron Gunderson.

I Can Only Imagine, Allen Frost, 2017. Five adventures of love and heartbreak dreamed in an imaginary world. Cover & color illustrations by Annabelle Barrett.

The Orphanage of Abandoned Teenagers, Allen Frost, 2017. A fictional guide for teens and their parents. Illustrated by the author.

In the Valley of Mystic Light: An Oral History of the Skagit Valley Arts Scene, 2017. A comprehensive illustrated tribute. Edited by Claire Swedberg & Rita Hupy.

Different Planet, Allen Frost, 2017. Four science fiction adventures: reincarnation, robots, talking animals, outer space and clones. Illustrated by Laura Vasyutynska.

Go with the Flow: A Tribute to Clyde Sanborn, 2018. Edited by Allen Frost. The life and art of a timeless river poet. In beautiful living color!

Homeless Sutra, Allen Frost, 2018. Four stories: Sylvan Moore, a flying monk, a water salesman, and a guardian rabbit.

The Lake Walker, Allen Frost 2018. A little novel set in black and white like one of those old European movies about death and life.

A Hundred Dreams Ago, Allen Frost, 2018. A winter book of poetry and prose. Illustrated by Aaron Gunderson.

Almost Animals, Allen Frost, 2018. A collection of linked stories, thinking about what makes us animals.

The Robotic Age, Allen Frost, 2018. A vaudeville magician and his faithful robot track down ghosts. Illustrated throughout by Aaron Gunderson.

Kennedy, Allen Frost, 2018. This sequel to *Roosevelt* is a coming-of-age fable set during two weeks in 1962 in a mythical Kennedyland. Illustrated throughout by Fred Sodt.

Fable, Allen Frost, 2018. There's something going on in this country and I can best relate it in fable: the parable of the rabbits, a bedtime story, and the diary of our trip to Ohio.

Elbows & Knees: Essays & Plays, Allen Frost, 2018. A thrilling collection of writing about some of my favorite subjects, from B-movies to Brautigan.

The Last Paper Stars, Allen Frost 2019. A trip back in time to the 20 year old mind of Frankenstein, and two other worlds of the future.

Walt Amherst is Awake, Allen Frost, 2019. The dreamlife of an office worker. Illustrated throughout by Aaron Gunderson.

When You Smile You Let in Light, Allen Frost, 2019. An atomic love story written by a 23 year old.

Pinocchio in America, Allen Frost, 2019. After 82 years buried underground, Pinocchio returns to life behind a car repair shop in America.

Taking Her Sides on Immortality, Robert Huff, 2019. The long awaited poetry collection from a local, nationally renowned master of words.

Florida, Allen Frost, 2019. Three days in Florida turned into a book of sunshine inspired stories.

Blue Anthem Wailing, Allen Frost, 2019. My first novel written in college is an apocalyptic, Old Testament race through American shadows while Amelia Earhart flies overhead.

The Welfare Office, Allen Frost, 2019. The animals go in and out of the office, leaving these stories as footprints.

Island Air, Allen Frost, 2019. A detective novel featuring haiku, a lost library book and streetsongs.

Imaginary Someone, Allen Frost, 2020. A fictional memoir featuring 45 years of inspirations and obstacles in the life of a writer.

Violet of the Silent Movies, Allen Frost, 2020. A collection of starry-eyed short story poems, illustrated by the author.

The Tin Can Telephone, Allen Frost, 2020. A childhood memory novel set in 1975 Seattle, illustrated by author.

Heaven Crayon, Allen Frost, 2020. How the author's first book *Ohio Trio* would look if printed as a Big Little Book. Illustrated by the author.

Old Salt, Allen Frost, 2020. Authors of a fake novel get chased by tigers. Illustrations by the author.

A Field of Cabbages, Allen Frost, 2020. The sequel to *The Robotic Age* finds our heroes in a race against time to save Sunny Jim's ghost. Illustrated by Aaron Gunderson.

River Road, Allen Frost, 2020. A paperboy delivers the news to a ghost town. Illustrated by the author.

The Puttering Marvel, Allen Frost, 2021. Eleven short stories with illustrations by the author.

Something Bright, Allen Frost, 2021. 106 short story poems walking with you from winter into spring. Illustrated by the author.

The Trillium Witch, Allen Frost, 2021. A detective novel about witches in the Pacific Northwest rain. Illustrated by the author.

Cosmonaut, Allen Frost, 2021. Yuri Gagarin's rocket lands in America. Midnight jazz, folk music, mystery and sorcery. Illustrated by the author.

Thriftstore Madonna, Allen Frost, 2021. 124 summer story poems. Illustrated by the author.

Half a Giraffe, Allen Frost, 2021. A magical novel about a counterfeiter and his unusual, beloved pet. Illustrated by the author.

Lexington Brown & The Pond Projector, Allen Frost, 2022. An underwater invention takes three friends through time. Illustrated by Aaron Gunderson.

The Robert Huck Museum, Allen Frost, 2022. The artist's life story told in photographs, woodcuts, paintings, prints and drawings.

Mrs. Magnusson & Friends, Allen Frost, 2022. A collection of 13 stories featuring mystery and ginkgo leaves.

Magic Island, Allen Frost, 2022. There's a memory machine in this magical novel that takes us to college.

A Red Leaf Boat, Allen Frost, 2022. Inspired by Japan, this book of 142 poems is the result of walking in autumn.

Forest & Field, Allen Frost, 2022. 117 forest and field recordings made during the summer months, ending with a lullaby.

The Wires and Circuits of Earth, Allen Frost, 2022. 11 stories from a train station pulp magazine.

The Air Over Paris, Allen Frost, 2023. This novel reveals the truth about semi-sentient speedbumps from Mars.

Neptunalia, Allen Frost, 2023. A movie-novel for Neptune, featuring mystery in a Counterfeit Reality machine. Illustrated by Aaron Gunderson.

The Worrys, Allen Frost, 2023. A family of weasels look for a better life and get it. Illustrated by Tai Vugia.

American Mantra, Allen Frost, 2023. The future needs poetry to sleep at night. Only one man and one woman can save the world. Illustrated by Robert Huck.

One Drop in the Milky Way, Allen Frost, 2023. A novel about retiring, with a little help from a skeleton and Abraham Lincoln.

Books by Bottom Dog Press

Ohio Trio, Allen Frost, 2001. Three short novels written in magic fields and small towns of Ohio. Reprinted as *Heaven Crayon* in 2020.

Bowl of Water, Allen Frost, 2004. Poetry. From the glass factory to when you wake up.

Another Life, Allen Frost, 2007. Poetry. From the last Ohio morning to the early bird.

Home Recordings, Allen Frost, 2009. Poetry. Dream machinery, filming Caruso, benign time travel.

The Mermaid Translation, Allen Frost, 2010. A bathysphere novel with Philip Marlowe.

Selected Correspondence of Kenneth Patchen, Edited by Larry Smith and Allen Frost, 2012. Amazing artist letters.

The Wonderful Stupid Man, Allen Frost, 2012. Short stories go from Aristotle's first car to the 500 dollar fool.